# Cuba after
# Communism

# Cuba after Communism

Eliana Cardoso
and
Ann Helwege

The MIT Press
Cambridge, Massachusetts
London, England

This book was set in Palatino by The MIT Press and printed and bound in the United States of America.

Library of Congress Cataloging-in-Publication Data

Cardoso, Eliana A.
    Cuba after communism / Eliana Cardoso and Ann Helwege.
        p.   cm.
    Includes bibliographical references and index.
    ISBN 0-262-03197-3
        1. Cuba—Politics and government—1959–   2. Communism—
    Cuba—History.   3. Cuba—Economic conditions—1959–   4. Cuba—
    Forecasting.   5. United States—Relations—Cuba.   6. Cuba—
    Relations—United States.   I. Helwege, Ann.   II. Title.
    F1788.C2575   1992
    303.48'27291023—dc20                                    92-5663
                                                             CIP

To Rudi and Stephen

# Contents

# Preface

Cuba is controversial. Many interpret its past and future through their own ideology, whether they endorse Castro's agenda or violently reject it. Can open-minded people identify common ground? Even those who honestly want to know what went right and what went wrong during the last thirty years of socialism in Cuba find it difficult to describe the basic facts of Cuba's social and economic experience. Not surprisingly, strong differences of opinion emerge.

For some, socialism spelled disaster from day one. Since then, nothing has changed: ". . . the island has stood still over the past thirty years, or even regressed in some major areas. . . "[1] This perspective portrays the Cuban economy as stagnant: "The country's gross national product today is more or less the same as it was in 1958, before the revolution. . . . On a per capita basis, it ranked third in the hemisphere in 1958; now it is considered one of the poorest countries in Latin America in per capita terms. . . . Productivity is also extremely low because the Cuban people refuse to work, in protest against the system."[2]

Other authors depict Cuba as dynamic, diversified, and the winner within Latin America in real economic growth in the 1970s and 1980s: "Cuba has the oldest and most developed economy, except for China, of the Third World socialist nations. As such, Cuba serves as an economic model, as well as a source of aid, guidance, and inspiration to many countries identifying with this expanding group."[3]

Propaganda there and biases here, and the shortage of data common to less developed countries, leave us with few hard facts on which to build a rigorous portrait of Cuban socialism, its merits, and its failings. All this is to say that this book will not meet with unanimous agreement. Some may not share our ideology, some will refuse to believe our evidence, and even some who accept the same facts will see progress where we see the end of the road.

Cuba is in crisis. This is no small setback that can be accommodated on the long road to socialism, where Che Guevara's "new man" will live beyond material desire. The conclusion we draw from Cuba's record is that the economy is collapsing for two reasons. First, the external environment that once sustained Cuba has disappeared virtually overnight. Support for Cuba, in trade and aid from the Soviet Union and its allies, is gone. In fact, with the rapid secession of one republic after another in late 1991, the Soviet Union is gone. What is left is sugar. Sugar is not easy to sell because most countries protect their domestic producers. The collapse of the East bloc economies has left Cuba in desperate need of new trade partners.

Second, centralized control prevents Cuba from adjusting to the shock of losing ties to the Soviet Union. Decentralization—and rewards for success—are the only effective means of using an economy's resources to maximum advantage. Even the fiercest repression cannot replicate the wonders of self-interest. Commitment to the common good and volunteerism seem to offer an alternative, but there is too little of it to change an increasingly gray, decaying scene.

Until Castro lessens restrictions on private production, Cubans will not scramble to fill in gaps in the output of food, housing, and basic goods. They cannot grow a few vegetables for sale without risking arrest. Nor can they create new industries, ranging from textiles to tourist trinkets, to displace the dominance of sugar in export earnings. The Cuban government courts foreign investors for joint ventures, particularly in tourism, but entrepreneurs are cautious about diving into a country where profit is a dirty word. Talking out of both sides of its mouth, the government assures foreign investors of high rates of return, but forbids Cubans to engage in "bourgeois" activities. The contradiction is more than theoretical: foreign firms are unsure of the rules of the game, and local entrepreneurs cannot participate. Investment and growth suffer.

The crisis is partly of Cuba's own making. It chose the losing side in a Cold War between superpowers. It alienated foreign capital by expropriating property, violating patents, and threatening to renege on its foreign debt. It also drove out its own entrepreneurs, intellectuals, and best-trained professionals, deriding them as traitors.

Even if we were to believe the claim that U.S. oppression is the sole cause of Cuba's problems, our basic conclusions would not change. Cuba gains nothing from facing off against the United States in an ideological battle. In the absence of Soviet help, Cuba needs access to the U.S. market and American tourists. And it needs private investment to finance structural change in an economy built on the assumption of trade with the Soviets. Before economic collapse does lasting damage, Cuba should build a new relationship with the United States. Cubans are unwilling to concede outright, but negotiations might lead to a face-saving peace.

There is much that is good in Cuba. Health, education, and economic equality are exemplary by Latin American standards. The debate will rage on whether this could be achieved in a free society, and if not, whether it is worth the price of repression. Today, these gains are at risk. Under socialism, economic decay makes it difficult to find the resources to maintain social welfare. With a transition to capitalism, the commitment to basic needs may evaporate.

We care deeply that Cuba's people have a soft landing. In a world that professes increasing enthusiasm for capitalism, socialist rhetoric adds to Cuba's isolation. It hinders access to markets and discourages investment needed for growth. A change in rhetoric alone would begin to open doors. Centralized control of assets must also give way to opportunities for Cubans to produce for profit, or adjustment will stall in the current stage of limited joint ventures between foreign firms and a rigid state apparatus. Finally, Cuban policymakers need to move beyond wishful thinking about a return to the past. They must move fast to design privatization schemes with some fairness, and they must identify aspects of social welfare that are most vulnerable in the years ahead.

Central to Cuba's future is Fidel Castro—hero, liberator, tyrant, terrorist. Much of what we know about him is of his own making: "Castro molds his own image as leader with exquisite care. In the space of seconds he can be terrible, human, cruel, amusing, transcendent."[4] He is widely viewed by the U.S. establishment as an enemy of the American people. In response to U.S. demands and Latin American cajoling, he has proved adamantly opposed to change. A change in leadership is due, although how it will be achieved is anyone's guess.

Where does U.S. policy fit in? The U.S. embargo compounds Cuba's economic and political isolation. In doing so, it stalls Cuban preparation for what seems an inevitable shift toward capitalism. Cuba's political, regulatory, and economic institutions do not synchronize with the needs of a market economy. Developing closer economic ties now will provide Cubans with some inkling of the challenge that lies ahead. Closer ties will also help to undermine Castro's hold on Cuban ideology.

Cuba is on our doorstep—even more so than Haiti. Economic crisis portends chaos and violent scapegoating. Dazed by the loss of economic ties to the Soviet Union, Cubans are still unsure of the mistakes made and whom to blame. A U.S. military invasion would ignite the flames of Cuban nationalism and rally crowds to Castro. Helping Cuba is far more important than overthrowing Castro. We must start negotiations before Cuba lands in our lap.

We want to thank Andy Zimbalist, Manuel Pastor, and Susan Eckstein, with whom we went to Cuba to find out firsthand what was achieved and what remains from better days. They disagree with many of our conclusions, but they cannot escape the fact that they helped us to form our opinion. The same is true of numerous Cuban academics, party members, and bureaucrats who showed us their achievements and failures. We suspect that they would not like to be associated with this book, and for that reason we do not mention their names.

We thank Moira Bucciarelli of The MIT Press, whose unwavering confidence got us through a round of rough challenge.

Rudi Dornbusch first suggested this project and helped us to develop policy recommendations. Rudi and Stephen babysat the book and the kids. Their notions about social justice and economic progress influenced our ideas. To both of them go our deepest thanks.

# Cuba after Communism

# 1

## Cuba's Quandary

In a few years at most, Cuba won't be Cuba—the sole socialist state in Latin America. A combination of forces, including the breakdown of international communism and the economic crisis, make its maverick socialist stance untenable over the long haul. This book explores prospects for the Cuban economy as it adjusts to domestic and global changes. We focus on three basic questions: What is the economic outlook for Cuba? How can the country minimize the costs of losing Soviet support? And what role should U.S. policy play in influencing Cuba's future?

The twentieth century has seen the conflict between communism and capitalism come full circle. The collapse of communism in Eastern Europe and in the Soviet Union represents a historical turning point, but ironically the concerns that initially nurtured communism have not disappeared. Communists abhorred poverty and wanted to abolish it. For "scientific" Marxists, the end of private property would encourage the development of a new citizen, driven not by private gain but by social benefit. Among less radical socialists, communism was an opinion about how the income of a country should be distributed. No doubt it advanced progress: without communism, China might have never found an answer to abject poverty, and Cuba's communism provided its poor with levels of health and education that they otherwise would not have achieved in the same period of time.[1]

Because communism failed to solve the problems of growth and freedom, it proved a poor response to dilemmas surrounding the question of how to allocate resources. But the distribution question still begs for an answer: How much should I have? How much should my neighbor have? Liberal democracy has never given a fully satisfactory answer to this question. The institutions under which we live, including our system of distributing income, keep changing. But dire poverty continues to exist in the midst of ostentatious wealth. The European Community, the United States, and Japan are islands of prosperity in a sea of unmet basic needs. Moreover, each of these nations harbors its own pockets of poverty. Environmentalists claim that billions of people cannot hope to enjoy the wealth of the few because natural resources limit economic growth. Thus, politics will have to focus on the distribution of what exists. The answer will not be an easy move toward unregulated free markets. That has been tried, and it failed a century ago.

The current crisis in Cuba poses the question of whether a good model of development exists. The angry rejection of socialism by those who endured its experiments rules out the communist utopia dreamed of by leftists during this century. But while socialism goes bankrupt in Cuba, other Latin American countries fail to join capitalism with social justice. Populism and profligacy have created economic chaos in many Latin American countries. Argentina, Brazil, and Peru are sad examples of instability and inequality. Cuba promises another macabre show even if its mistakes are of a different nature. Now that outside help and trade have vanished, socialist orthodoxy will impose tragic sacrifices on the Cuban people.

Will a conservative, anticommunist revolution unravel the social progress of thirty years? We hope not. The Cuban exile community is beginning to put its weight behind the idea of a Cuban solution based on dialogue. Proposals call for participation by representatives of the Cuban government, the exile community, internal opposition groups, and international observers. The talk is no longer of overthrowing Castro, but of promoting the conditions for change. Yet the conservative agenda for change does not spell out ways to moderate the social costs of a transition to capitalism.

This book develops a pragmatic vision toward which Cubans should now strive. It offers no alternative utopia: socialism does not deliver the goods, and capitalism does not distribute them fairly. To expect that Cuba will find a better way is perhaps to believe in fairy tales. But without some hope that capitalism can have a more humanitarian face, we could not have written this book.

**Imminent Change**

Cuba is a small island of 44,000 square miles, only 90 miles from the Florida Keys (see figure 1.1), densely populated by 11 million people, and too specialized in the production of sugar. These are among the few undisputed facts about Cuba. On all the rest, the literature is marked by ideological dogmatism from both ends of the political spectrum.

A dispassionate evaluation of Cuba's development is difficult because even estimating Cuban growth or comparing it to data from market economies is controversial. Nonetheless, evidence supports the claim that, until 1985, Cuba experienced substantial economic growth along with distributional equity. This good performance was made possible with generous Soviet aid.

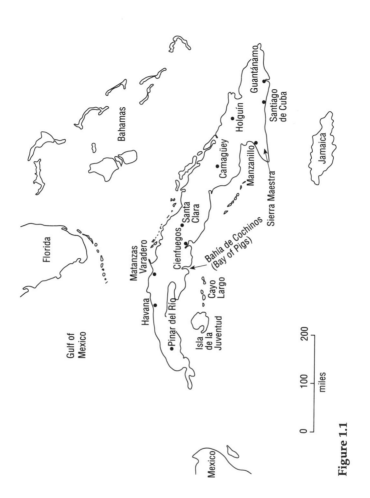

**Figure 1.1**

Cuban health performance is unparalleled in Latin America. Infant mortality is below that in many U.S. cities. Moreover, all Cubans can read and write. But regrettably, there is little worth reading. By 1991 the bookshops were empty, both because of censorship and a lack of paper on which to print. Fidel Castro's revolution was then entering its thirty-third year beset by shortages of food and consumer goods.

Unlike Eastern Europe's fallen dictators, Fidel Castro was once a genuine revolutionary leader. Many Cubans still admire him. Others do not even respect him, although they value Cuba's education and health services. As people stand in bread lines, their resentment shifts to Castro's reputed senility, the inefficiencies of socialism, and the well-advertised scapegoat, the U.S. embargo. No one is happy with the situation, but there is no consensus about where to pin the blame.

Between 1986 and 1991, output per capita and labor productivity declined; the government's budget deficit increased eightfold; average wages stagnated, and housing construction dwindled. In response to the crisis, the state has tightened its control over production and distribution. Market-oriented mechanisms, which allowed private sales of some food, housing and artisan services between 1976 and 1985, have been eliminated.

Cuba's task is made harder because the economy is so ill-equipped to compete in world trade. The productive capacity is geared largely to sugar. Although sugar accounts for just 4 percent of Cuba's Global Social Product (GSP), it accounts for three quarters of Cuba's exports.[2] The world price of sugar has been depressed for years, and the U.S. trade embargo has excluded Cuba from its potential market. As the former Soviet Union's crisis deepens, problems multiply in shipping sugar to the republics and oil to Cuba. At the same time, China is planning to expand cultivation of its own beet and sugar cane, and Cuba's trade with the former socialist countries in Eastern Europe is dwindling to nothing. The decline in trade with the East bloc has forced Cuba into a crisis worse than that faced by other Latin American countries after the debt shock.

Autarky is not a sound solution. The country depends completely on imports of wheat, the key staple of consumption. Its industry relies on foreign inputs ranging from soap to plastics to spare parts. In 1991, oxen were used to replace tractors. Bicycles were the alternative to idle cars and buses that lacked gasoline. A small, open economy like Cuba's needs trade to avert a dramatic fall in its standard of living.

As the Soviet Union abandons its former ally, Cuba's overtures to Latin America are largely ignored. European countries, once tolerant of Cuba's rebelliousness, are now hardening their stance because they are paying the bill for decades of misdirected socialism in the East. A few multinational companies, eager to secure an early foothold in the potentially lucrative tourism sector, are talking business. But even if joint ventures in tourism and agro-industry successfully generate hard currency some years ahead, things will certainly get worse in the short run. A new term, "zero option," has entered the vocabulary of survival on the island; Castro now exhorts Cubans to prepare for a virtual absence of any imports. Havana, once the most opulent town in the Caribbean, is slowly crumbling while people line up for food or leave the country.

Partly because Castro now prefers to see dissidents flee to Miami than create trouble at home, he has little internal opposition. It takes just a few hours to reach Florida from Havana by yacht, but a *tubero* (a person who uses a raft made of tire tubes, planks, and plastic sheeting) can drift at sea for days before being rescued by the U.S. Coast Guard. Only half of tuberos survive storms and winds. Nonetheless, more than one thousand of them reached Florida in the first half of 1991.

Cuba has been calm to date, but an economy going nowhere, desertion by the brightest, restless youth, and an aging
leader make for a potentially explosive political situation.
At present there are few signs of organized opposition. In
1991 a record number of Cubans—about 100,000—volun-
teered to plant crops as part of a government plan to become
food self-sufficient.[3] Many felt compelled to sign up to keep
their jobs or unemployment benefits, but neither the pressure
to farm nor a squeeze on labor before the Pan-American
Games produced the widely anticipated protests. Nationalism runs strong among Cubans, and few are eager to bow to
pressure by the U.S. government. Castro may scrape through
for a year, perhaps a few years. But eventually, the collapsing
standard of living will give way to change.

## Small Steps in the Wrong Direction

Entangled in his own rhetoric, Castro seems unable to open
the economy, but incongruously seems to believe that foreign
investors will bail out the country. As the government clamps
down on most small entrepreneurs, deriding them as petite
bourgeoisie, it aggressively seeks joint ventures with multinational corporations. New hotels are springing up on the
beach at Varadero, and oil companies are sought to prospect
along Cuba's coast. Fisheries, telecommunications, light industry, pharmaceuticals, and construction already have joint
ventures and production-sharing agreements in place. But if
an enterprising Cuban casts a line into the sea for profit, he
will face arrest.

The fundamental issue in Cuban economic adjustment is
whether it is feasible for a socialist economy to work under
a partially market-driven system. A socialist economy forbids
the ownership of the means of production by individuals.
What does this prohibition entail in a period of transition?

Introducing markets for some goods will bring in only a crippled market mechanism. Economic incentives can push workers to produce more within existing enterprises, but as long as profits are prohibited, new ventures will be slow to appear. State ownership slows the mobility of capital from one sector to another, as firms face neither the risk of failure nor the rewards of success.

Markets and price signals need private ownership and competition to work. Higher prices both signal scarcity to consumers and spur producers to increase their output. The prohibition of private ownership aims at achieving equality, but foreign investors follow terms set by international rates of profit. Ironically, the economic distance between Cuban workers and foreign investors increases when the Cuban government has to sweeten joint venture deals with low wages. The Spanish, the French, and the Japanese can be shareholders, but Cubans cannot. How long will Cubans accept the contradictions of this mixed system?

The fervor for independence in Latin America in the early nineteenth century is often attributed to successful local *creoles* resenting the right of Spanish-born *peninsulares* to hold office: now locals can hold office, but only foreigners can make money. Economic apartheid extends to consumption as well. Night-clubs and bars that retain the flavor of Havana's hey-day and new beach resorts only serve those holding dollars, which Cubans cannot carry. While a few Europeans toast with sauternes the opening of their jointly owned hotels in Varadero, Cubans must wonder why they cannot open their own hotels and celebrate with *mojitos*.[4]

Joint ventures and tourism still play only a small role in the economy, but the problems of socialism extend throughout the system. Bureaucrats determine whether Cubans buy bread or rice, whether they play tapes of Madonna or Los Van Van, and whether hair dyes for sale this week come in blonde or brunette. Despite their relative isolation, Cubans are plugged into world culture. They make complicated arrangements for a friend-of-a-cousin to bring in blue jeans, tape decks, and tampons. Confiscations at customs provide market research for the central planning board, but it isn't translated into production decisions.

Failure to take advantage of the incentives built into capitalism means that not only are there shortages of luxuries, but food is scarcer than it need be. Peasant markets, which flourished briefly in the late 1970s and early 1980s, were eliminated because a few *campesinos* became rich. Instead, eggs are rationed, meat is almost nonexistent, and fruits and vegetables are scarce. Lack of food in the tropics is often the result of bad policy: how can bananas and coconuts be in short supply where they will grow like weeds?

Cubans are not starving, but residents of a country that claims to be the richest in Latin America can reasonably expect more than three ounces of bread per day. As the Soviets reduce their trade with Cuba, grain will become even scarcer. Tight restrictions on private production exacerbate the burden of diminishing foreign aid.

## Replacing the System

Cuba's adherence to socialism makes it a pariah of Latin American leaders, whose rhetoric is aimed at securing free-trade agreements with the United States. Five years ago, Cuba enjoyed cooperative relations with most capitalist countries. Now that the United States is the ringleader of the only game in town, relations are cooling. Lucrative commercial deals will always find a buyer. But Cuba can count on less aid from Spain, more difficult access to the Brazilian politicians who buy vaccines, and hesitancy from leaders in former Soviet republics to open their doors to Cuban representatives. Socialist rhetoric, in a world dominated by free-market ideology, forces Cuba toward autarky. Yet the country cannot function in economic isolation.

As bilateral free-trade agreements displace GATT negotiations, Cuba risks losing entry into newly forming trade megablocks. Europe has taken major steps toward economic unification in 1992. Mexico, the United States, and Canada are negotiating the North American Free Trade Agreement; and Argentina, Brazil, and Uruguay have formed the "Mercosur." Cuba needs access to markets to unload sugar that the East bloc once bought. And it needs relief from protectionist barriers within these blocs if it is to develop new exports, such as pharmaceuticals and electronics, which take advantage of its cheap skilled labor. The payoff of switching to capitalism and joining negotiations with Western markets is high.

Attracting capital to modernize and expand Cuba's productive capacity requires privatization. Joint ventures alone will not do the job. Cuba needs more than big hotels; it needs everything from hot-dog stands to fax machine outlets. Small firms are essential to growth. It is simply not possible for the government to negotiate complex deals with thousands of entrepreneurs.

Substantial private investment requires that Cuba play by the capitalist rules of the game: clear private property rights, enforcement of contracts, stable exchange rates, prices that are not subject to arbitrary political changes, and a reliable physical infrastructure. How the Cuban government sets up the rules of the game will determine who is willing to play, and how much money the players will put up. Unfortunately, with the end of the Cold War Cuba is no longer strategically attractive. The United States will cough up relatively little money to help Cuba make the transition to capitalism. Cuba will have to earn a living, through high quality, competitively priced exports, and tourism. There is a long distance from the current situation to a viable market economy.

## What Kind of Transition?

Castro's government still holds enough power to influence a shift toward capitalism. For now, there are no signs that Castro will relent in his stubborn adherence to socialism. His current stance drags out an era of economic decline. Rising frustration is bound to polarize the country and make a bloody transition more likely; running the economy into the ground may well discredit the social welfare achievements of the revolution.

The notion that Cuba faces a trade-off between socialist gains and capitalist growth is false. Cuban socialism was effective in overcoming the dire poverty that prevailed in the 1950s. Castro seized a historic opportunity to parlay Cuba's strategic position into prosperity during the Cold War. To his credit, he directed the benefits to the poor. The state is now no longer in a position to distribute the benefits of trade with the Soviet Union; instead, it must find ways to generate income to avert economic collapse.

Eager to get rid of a system that inhibits growth, Cubans could throw out the baby with the bath water and embrace an ultraconservative government bent on laissez-faire. Experience with authoritarianism in Latin America has shown that (contrary to popular myth) repression and a regulatory free-for-all do not foster growth. States that abdicate responsibility for redistributing income, setting rules of fair play in markets, and creating a stable macroeconomic environment inevitably face political chaos. Cuba must avoid trading one bad system for another.

By Latin American standards, Castro looks squeaky clean. He has wisely avoided the purchase of designer eyeglasses, and charges of corruption are minimal. He has an unwavering compassion for his people. Does he have the will to direct a peaceful transition toward capitalism? Only Cubans can guide the extent to which socialism's accomplishments—low infant mortality, access to daycare, universal health care—will not be lost in the process of change. Finding a leader who is tough enough to manage the transition and make it fair will not be easy.

The political legitimacy of a shift to capitalism will be made harder by the fact that growth will not take off instantly. Cuba is still an economy that depends on sugar exports, with a long waiting list for phones and a stock of cars that includes a few classics and a lot of junk. Finding new markets for sugar, creating infrastructure, and diversifying production will take time.

## U.S. Policy

There are 1 million Cuban-Americans in the United States. Cuban exiles have done well, and U.S. policy toward Cuba is in good measure shaped by lobbyists from Miami. The Cuban American Foundation is an efficient anti-Castro machine. Yet its dominance is beginning to change, with *dialogueros* (Cuban-Americans who criticize the revanchism of an older era) playing an increasingly important role. Family ties have been strengthened by charter flights that ferry relatives between the island and Miami. An invasion is no longer seen as the only option. Solidarity and the interests of the Cuban people may now come first.

On May 20, 1991, President George Bush called for free elections in Cuba under international observation and the release of political prisoners: "Freedom and democracy, Mr.

Castro! Not sometime, not some day, but now!" He suggested that if Cuba stops subverting its neighbors, U.S.-Cuban relations could improve significantly, but President Bush has yet to take steps toward a dialogue. The current policy of isolation gives Castro the benefit of painting the United States as Cuba's oppressor. The embargo alone is fairly characterized as the equivalent of economic warfare, and it provides a justification for rationing and restrictions on individual activity. How should U.S. policy toward Cuba change now that the Cold War is over?

Negotiations toward an opening of trade relations and creative diplomacy might help to draw Cuba out of its shell. A policy of isolation prevents the United States from influencing the future of Cuba and excludes U.S. firms from joint ventures that now give other foreigners a foothold in the Cuban economy. Now that Cuba no longer poses a military threat to the United States, even conservatives must be asking if the blockade serves our interests.

As the largest country in the Caribbean, Cuba offers potentially important leadership in a region beset by poverty and instability. Helping to restart economic growth in Cuba could do more than the Caribbean Basin Initiative has done in ten years. Cuba will need assistance in moving away from central planning. U.S. aid can play an important role in ensuring that chaos does not replace the crumbling socialist system. Cuba's monetary system has no credibility, the government budget is deeply in the red, and diversification away from sugar requires heavy investment. Aid would have a positive impact on all three fronts. The United States should begin talks and help to shape a better future for Cubans. Gleefully watching as Cuba collapses simply means more Cubans in Miami and another decade of trouble in the Caribbean. Who needs another Haiti?

# 2    Struggles: Past and Present

## Independence, So-Called

Cuba's most enduring hero, José Martí, inspired Cuba's struggle for independence from Spain. Ten years of war between these two nations in the 1870s had proved fruitless for Cuba. When fighting broke out again in 1895, Americans chafed at the bit. They, not the Spaniards, were the dominant economic force in Cuba. The mysterious sinking of the USS *Maine* provided a rationale for U.S. intervention in 1898. (See table 2.1 for important dates in Cuba's recent history.) After a death toll of some 300,000 came formal independence, but the strings of the Platt amendment bound the island to U.S. control. This treaty granted the United States the right to intervene militarily, to control Cuba's debts and treaties with other countries, and to establish naval bases on Cuban land. Nationalists found little solace in the island's new status as a U.S. protectorate.

Economic bonds ran deep. U.S. goods received preferential tariff treatment in Cuba, and U.S. firms dominated investments. By 1928, U.S. firms controlled about 75 percent of the sugar cane crop. Cuba not only gained access to the U.S. sugar market, where crop supports kept prices high, but with the

**Table 2.1**
Important dates in Cuba's recent history

| | |
|---|---|
| 1898–1901 | The United States occupies Cuba. |
| 1934 | The Platt Amendment is abrogated, formally ending U.S. rights to intervene in Cuba. |
| 1953 | Fidel Castro leads an unsuccessful revolt against Fulgencio Batista's dictatorship. |
| 1956 | Castro begins new revolt against Batista. |
| 1959 | Batista is overthrown: Castro takes power. |
| 1961 | Bay of Pigs invasion by U.S.-backed anti-Castro exiles ends in defeat. |
| 1962 | Cuban Missile Crisis. |
| 1967 | Cuban leader Ernesto "Che" Guevara killed by government forces while leading guerrillas in Bolivia. |
| 1975 | Cuban troops sent to Angola. |
| 1980 | Mariel boat lift: Castro sends several thousand criminals and mental patients to the United States. |
| 1988 | Cuba signs agreement to withdraw from Angola. |
| 1989 | Withdrawal from Angola begins. Castro opposes Glasnost and Perestroika. Castro upstages Gorbachev during the Soviet leader's visit to Havana. |
| 1990 | Economy severely deteriorates with curtailment of Soviet aid. |

help of Great Britain the United States formed a consumer cartel, which prohibited the sale of Cuban sugar to other countries. Cuba was a one-crop economy tied to one buyer.

Revolutionary fervor struck again in the 1930s, an era in which Leon Trotsky, an advocate of world revolution, found sanctuary in Mexico under the progressive president, Lázaro Cárdenas. Cuban communists and nationalists challenged Gerardo Machado's despotism and U.S. dominance.[1] A socialist president, Ramón Grau San Martín, attempted to cut the workday to eight hours, grant land to peasants, and limit foreign ownership. A U.S.-backed coup d'etat, led by Fulgencio Batista, ended attempts at reform. With its grip on Cuba as percent had running water. With 70 percent of farmland concentrated in the hands of 8 percent of landowners, cane cutters were lucky to survive the 'dead season' between harvests. Even urban Cubans were unhappy with the extremes of government corruption and brutality. The fight against the Batista dictatorship had the sympathy of many Cuban elites and U.S. policymakers.

In 1959 Fidel Castro overthrew Batista after two years of guerrilla warfare in the Sierra Maestra of southeast Cuba. Although the U.S. ambassador to Cuba personally supported Batista, the State Department imposed an embargo on shipments of arms to the Cuban government. The United States was eager to end political chaos under Batista. Resistance to Batista came from all quarters, including moderate urban elites, whom the United States expected would gain power after the revolution. Castro's elusive politics barely influenced policy. Even the State Department's own Cuban specialist, William Wieland, a strong opponent of Batista, admitted, "Fidel Castro is surrounded by commies. I don't know whether he is himself a communist. . . [But] I am certain he is subject to communist influences."[5]

By 1961, Fidel had disbanded prerevolutionary interest groups. He also declared himself a Marxist-Leninist, postponed free-elections, began a sweeping land reform, and nationalized the education system. Thirty-three years after the revolution he remains the sole leader of a one-party state.

## External Events

The divorce from the United States cost Cuba dearly. In 1960, the United States canceled Cuba's sugar quota and placed an embargo on all nonfood and nonmedical trade with Cuba. In 1961, anti-Castro Cuban exiles failed in a U.S.-backed attempt to invade Cuba in the Bay of Pigs. In 1962, the embargo was

firm as ever, the United States sought to pacif
sentiment by agreeing in 1934 to abrogate the F
ment.

By the 1950s, U.S. companies controlled two of t
refineries, more than 90 percent of the telephone a
utilities, 50 percent of the public railroads, the enti
industry, most of the tourist industry, 40 of the
mills, and seven of the ten largest agricultural enter
1959, the book value per Cuban of U.S. enterprises
($143) was more than three times that of the rest
America.[3] But U.S. dominance had a counterpart in
dependence. Lack of industrial development before th
lution is often attributed to the duty-free access of i
from the United States. The benefits of close ties to the
were not all one-sided: Cuba sold sugar to the United
at prices well above the world price.

Cuba's concessional access to the U.S. sugar market w
important source of aid before the revolution. Even if t
relations are normalized in the future, Cuba may not s
return of this privilege. U.S. sugar producers held (and
hold) enough political power to close out foreign competit
Under the Sugar Act of 1934, the Department of Agricultu
set import quotas on foreign sugar, and until 1960 Cuba ha
the largest quota. Thus Cuba sold sugar to the United State
at prices that were often as much as 60 percent above worl
prices.

Americans loved Havana, and Cuban economic performance looked at least as good as the average in Latin America.
More Cadillacs were reputedly sold in Havana in 1954 than
in any other city in the world.[4] Per capita ownership of
televisions was the highest in Latin America, and 87 percent
of urban homes had electricity. Rural Cubans did not fare so
well: two thirds lived in shacks with dirt floors, and only 2

tightened to include all goods, with a provision to bar aid to countries trading with Cuba.

Lured by new U.S. aid initiatives, including establishment of the Alliance for Progress and the Inter-American Development Bank, the rest of Latin America fell into line with U.S. efforts to ostracize Castro. A promise to "make the Andes the Sierra Maestra of Latin America" did little to win Castro friends in high places, particularly once Che Guevara's 1967 campaign in Bolivia proved that this was no idle talk.

Cuba's expulsion from the Organization of American States (OAS) in 1962 marked the beginning of its diplomatic isolation. By 1965, only Mexico and Canada in the Western Hemisphere recognized the Castro government. OAS sanctions against Cuba were lifted in 1975, however, and relations have since been restored with all countries in the region except the United States.

The Soviet Union and the Eastern bloc countries filled the trade gap created by U.S. sanctions. By 1962, communist countries were absorbing 82 percent of Cuba's exports, despite surpluses of sugar in the Eastern bloc. Eager to secure a beachhead in the Caribbean, the Warsaw Pact absorbed large trade deficits.

Beginning in 1976, President Jimmy Carter attempted to gradually normalize relations between the United States and Cuba. But in 1980, relations soured with the Mariel boatlift, an exodus of 125,000 Cubans that occurred when restrictions on emigration were eased. Castro exploited the situation by putting prisoners and the mentally ill on the boats. Tension increased further in the early 1980s when President Ronald Reagan accused Castro of supplying arms to leftists in Central America, and again in 1985 when Washington's Radio Marti went on the air. In late 1987, a breakthrough allowed for an agreement reinstating immigration procedures.

Many Cuban-Americans would like to see Castro dead. The United States demands that Cuba release political prisoners and pay compensation for nationalized U.S. companies, worth roughly $1 billion in 1960. For Cuba to do so would be to accept the system that predated the revolution as fair. Meanwhile, Cuba urges the United States to relax the trade embargo and dismantle its military base on the island. Can they strike a deal?

## At Home

From Fidel Castro's victory in 1959 until 1970, the Cuban revolution ran under his personal leadership. The year 1970 marked both his first dramatic failure—that of achieving the ambitious goal of a 10-million-ton sugar cane harvest—and the beginning of formalized political institutions in government. In 1972 the Executive Committee took on more authority over agencies and ministries. The Communist Party, formally established in 1965, held its first congress in 1975. A new constitution was adopted in 1976, establishing an election process for municipal assemblies that ultimately determine the makeup of the National Assembly. From a situation in which Castro ruled by fiat, the system has evolved into one in which he "interprets" legislation. Despite an electoral process, organized opposition is not tolerated from within or outside the party apparatus. In theory, the system works on the notion of popular consensus. Even Castro's most ardent admirers base his legitimacy on his brilliance rather than on the democratic process (see box 2.1).

Given the difficulty of replicating Cuba's economic relationship with the Soviet Union, the system has never made a case for efficiency under centralized rule. Attempts at socialism in Chile under Allende and in Nicaragua under the Sandinistas collapsed in part because the Soviets did not

**Box 2.1**
**The Last Communist?**
Despite cancer and a heart attack, Fidel Castro is as tough in his old age as he seemed in his youth. He spent his childhood near the eastern town of Biran, where sugar companies were opening virgin forest for cane. His father, Angel Castro, an immigrant from Spain, detested the United States for its intervention in Cuba's war of independence. Angel also had no taste for taxes or legal property deeds, and his wealth grew rapidly through questionable claims on land.

Illiteracy and poverty ran rampant in the Oriente. Castro was sent to Belén to study with the Jesuits, where he became known as an outstanding athlete, scholar, and rabble-rouser. His penchant for taking the lead followed him to the University of Havana, where he joined the violent political gangs of the 1940s. He was suspected of several shootings that served to settle disputes between rival leaders. In 1947, outfitted with a submachine gun and a pistol, Castro joined an abortive invasion of the Dominican Republic. The following year he turned up in Colombia and was accused of inciting the riots that erupted after the shooting of Jorge Gaitán.

Castro's first daring attempt to overthrow the Cuban government took the form of a badly outnumbered attack on the Moncada barracks in Santiago de Cuba. With better luck than most of his comrades, Castro survived and landed in jail. His trial and brilliant speech, "History Will Absolve Me," turned him into a national hero.

Amnesty brought him freedom and he went to Mexico to prepare the revolution. In late 1956, he set sail from Veracruz on the yacht *Granma* for Cuba. Eighty-two men crossed on a boat meant for ten, but shortly after their arrival a military ambush reduced them to twenty. Charisma and the injustices of prerevolutionary Cuba helped to overcome the odds, as peasants in the Sierra Maestra rallied to Castro's support. Fast talk created the illusion of a large force, and urban raids by allied groups convinced Habaneros that change was possible. With Batista's fall in 1959, Castro became Cuba's hope for redemption.

Today Castro stands at the brink and gambles with his country's future. His self-confidence has not wavered. Still, Castro might recall the words of General Cantillo, as he came out of Batista's office on December 22, 1958: "Every time I read the life of a great man, I skip the last pages because the end is always disagreeable."[6]

deliver enough aid to quell internal strife and offset U.S. hostility. Neither Cuba's economy nor its political system stand as models for Latin Americans to emulate. Nonetheless, Cuba is better off than Central American economies such as Guatemala, Honduras, and Panama. As of 1990, all Cubans could read, were well fed, and had good health care. Cuban life expectancy was seventy-five years. Over 70 percent of families had television sets. There were none of the signs of abject poverty that one finds in the slums of Latin America. But even before the recent crisis, Havana was no paradise. Much of Havana is crumbling, and housing is a major problem. Ration books once guaranteed access to basic commodities at fixed prices, but now they do not even do that.

## Ideology versus Pragmatism

After the liquidation of capitalism and a short attempt at introducing centralized planning, the Sino-Guevarist model—idealistic and based on political mobilization of the masses—had its turn. Che Guevara's economic philosophy, with its stress on the creation of a new 'socialist man,' promised to raise worker productivity without material incentives. Volunteerism, the cornerstone of Cuban socialism, proved inadequate in getting the cane cut.

Hardliners in the Communist Party, partisans of a Stalinist centrally planned model spiced with Sino-Guevarism, have repeatedly confronted advocates of a more flexible and pragmatic model. As a consequence, economic policies have undergone frequent shifts. The 1970s brought material incentives and some markets in a moderate version of the pre-Gorbachev Soviet reform model (the System of Direction and Planning of the Economy, SDPE). Peasant markets were briefly encouraged in the early 1980s. But Castro shifted again in 1982 and began to criticize peasant markets and self-employment. In

1984 he appointed a group of loyalists who took away planning functions from the Central Planning Board (JUCEPLAN). In 1986, Fidel Castro announced the Rectification Process, an attempt to reinforce socialism. Policymakers reversed gear, backing away from decentralization and market mechanisms, returning to the Guevarist model. The Rectification Process represents a thrust in the exact opposite direction of current reforms in Eastern Europe.

## The 1960s

In the 1960s, the state collectivized all means of production and services except 20 percent of agricultural land, 2 percent of transportation, a small number of fishing cooperatives, and some personal services. The agrarian reform, first decreed in 1959, had an important redistributive impact. Extension of reforms in 1963 reduced maximum holdings to 65 hectares (163 acres) and placed all expropriated property in state ownership. Prior to the revolution, most land was held in large plantations worked by wage labor. The state-owned farm, with workers receiving wages, became the dominant agricultural organization. Family plots within state farms were eliminated in 1967; land has been gradually fused into collective plots that are cultivated by brigades. The government determines which crops are to be planted and sets production quotas and prices for state and private farms. The state's goal has been to eliminate remaining private farms by purchasing the land when owners die or retire, or by encouraging individual farmers to join state farms.[7]

The early 1960s were marked by optimism about Cuba's potential agricultural and industrial diversification. To break the dominance of sugar, cane was uprooted to make room for corn, rice, cotton, tomatoes, and new crops like soybeans. Sugar production fell from 5.9 million tons in 1959 to just 3.8

million tons in 1963. This loss, however, was not accompanied by the anticipated success of non-export crops. In fact, rice, corn, and millet production each fell by at least 25 percent.[8] Several explanations exist for the failure of early attempts at diversification: agrarian reform disrupted planting and harvesting; shortages of labor developed because of opportunities in the military and higher rural incomes, which eased the need to work long hours; rural workers lacked familiarity with nonsugar crops; and the weather did not help. Sugar prices spiked in 1963, leading to the "great debate," in which arguments for specialization in sugar prevailed. Cuban planners abandoned agricultural diversification and concentrated on sugar trade with the Soviets.

In industry, shortages of materials and spare parts led to frequent shutdowns in the pharmaceutical, textile. and ceramic industries. Cubans improvised, often to the dismay of supervisors, by cannibalizing equipment to keep other machines running. By 1962, the Soviets and East Europeans were installing new plants. However, fewer than 18 percent of Cubans had achieved the sixth grade before the revolution, and among those who did, emigration rates were high. Lack of skilled technicians thus hurt early industrial growth.

Che Guevara argued that people fully liberated from the chains of capitalism would work because work is an integral part of the human experience. The "new man" would act as a member of a society of equals and work hard, not for personal material reward but for the good of society. His opponents, who favored material incentives within socialism, argued that there should be more pay for those who worked harder and longer. Reason did not prevail, and proponents of moral incentives won the debate in 1965. They proceeded to convert Cubans into new socialist men through mobilization and education. Their failure was widely acknowledged.

Idealists started talking about the long road from socialism to communism.

New methods were launched. The country was reorganized along a military model. In 1969 it became mandatory for all workers to have a workforce control card that contained their productivity, political views, and employment history. Any worker wishing to change jobs needed the permission of a regional officer of the labor ministry.

The difficulties of the 1960s culminated in the unrealistic goal of a 10-million-ton sugar harvest by 1970. Despite an enormous sacrifice of resources in other sectors, only 8.5 million tons of sugar were harvested. More than an economic failure, this represented a devastating symbolic defeat.

## The 1970s

With few goods to buy, material incentives discredited, and moral incentives glorified, the "old man" reacted by cutting labor effort. Absenteeism and economic debacle forced a return to the Soviet path. In 1973 the pendulum swung toward material incentives for exemplary work, some wage differentials, prizes, and awards in kind. Incentives included preferred status for new housing, a refrigerator, or a vacation.

Prices continued to be fixed by the government, which limited the prices of basic foodstuffs and essential manufactures to protect low-income groups. Prices of most goods remained largely unchanged for two decades after they were frozen in the early 1960s. Increasingly, prices bore no relationship to costs or to world prices. Shortages of goods meant less incentive to work for monetary rewards.

Nonetheless, the 1970s are considered the heyday of Cuban economic growth. World sugar prices more than tripled between 1970 and 1975. Conservatives claim that Soviet aid skyrocketed; some of this increase reflects higher prices paid for sugar, which rose from 6 cents a pound in 1970 to more than 30 cents throughout the late 1970s.[9] Cuba joined the Council for Mutual Economic Assistance (Comecon) in 1972, securing long-term economic links to Eastern Europe. In 1975 Cuban-Soviet military collaboration began with the arrival of Cuban troops in Africa. Cuba initiated aid to Angola; the U.S.S.R. pressed for joint intervention in Ethiopia, where Cuba stationed 13,000 troops in 1979.

At home, investment increased rapidly. According to Zimbalist and Brundenius, the value of gross investment nearly tripled between 1970 and 1975.[10] In the latter half of the decade, new sugar mills and terminals, a cement plant, and a textile plant were put in place. Plants and petroleum refineries were modernized. Yet both sugar and nickel production stagnated; annual production of sugar averaged 6.8 million tons between 1976 and 1980.

A parallel market was introduced in 1973, in which surplus goods produced by state enterprises were sold at a price three to eight times higher than their price in the rationed market. This was evidently introduced principally to soak up excess liquidity caused by static prices in the rationed market. In 1980 a dramatic experiment in free peasant markets allowed private small holders to sell surplus food at market prices. For the first time, farmers had a mechanism to reap rewards for higher production. And although consumers complained about prices, more food was available.

**The 1980s**

Artisan and housing markets were introduced in the first half of the 1980s. New housing laws allowed tenants to become owners, private self-employment was permitted, and access to construction materials became easier. Combined with state help, the result was a strong housing construction boom.

A collapse of sugar prices, coupled with the fiscal and external payments deficits, plunged Cuba's economy into crisis in 1982. Desperate for hard currency, Havana issued a foreign investment code to attract joint ventures with the state. It also clamped down on a burgeoning free market, where a new class of middlemen was growing rich and craftsmen were hiring workers to produce goods using raw materials stolen from state enterprises. Even in the absence of theft, private production was competing with the state for productive resources. Mixing socialism with market mechanisms was declared a failure.

The free market, regarded as a temporary formula to resolve pressing problems, was banned in 1986 when the Mao-Guevarist model staged a comeback with the Rectification Process. Material incentives were blamed for corrupting the workers, reverting socialism to capitalism, and eroding revolutionary fervor. Cubans then saw a reinforcement of controls and closer scrutiny of their prizes and bonuses. The relative decentralization of fixing norms and wages was revamped. Housing rules were modified to impede activities that Castro condemned; laws that permitted people to enrich themselves through construction for sale were changed. Peasant markets were abolished.

The 1986 return to Guevarist principles derives in part from ideological efforts to revive socialism. The use of voluntary labor in the form of minibrigades has become increasingly important, particularly in the construction sector. So, too, has the use of special-force brigades made up of highly committed workers, whose members receive better food and a higher salary than ordinary workers.

The Rectification Process is also the result of Castro's political struggle to retain power. And it is an attempt to cope with economic problems. Except for a brief spike in 1980, world sugar prices were abysmally low throughout the decade. A decline in imports from the Soviet Union in 1986 also marked the beginning of the end in Cuba's economic relations with Comecon members. After 1989, trade dwindled rapidly.

## How Much Growth?

Everything about Cuba is subject to controversy. Among academics, Cuba's economic growth generates much of the debate. Cuban growth is at best an educated guess based on different estimates and incomplete information. The thorniest problem resides in the Cuban system of accounting—the system of material balances—common to the Soviet trading bloc. Capitalist countries use a national accounting method based on value-added, known as gross domestic product (GDP), to avoid double counting and to obtain the value of all final goods and services produced in a country. By contrast, Cuba's standard measure of the total flow of goods produced by the economy is the global social product (GSP). Its value is not calculated on a value-added basis, and it excludes services such as education, health, defense, culture, housing, and public administration, but includes the physical inputs these services use. GSP, in principle, is not very different from GDP. But the problem does not end with methodological differences. The use of administered (rather than market) prices complicates the picture. Scholars disagree on which prices to use to value goods to accurately add them up.

Official Cuban statistics point to real per capita growth between 1970 and 1985 in excess of 7 percent per year, a remarkable performance both by Latin American and Asian standards. Who believes it? World Bank and Central Intelligence Agency (CIA) estimates of Cuban economic growth were dismal until the late 1970s, but because their figures became controversial, the World Bank stopped publishing them. Mesa-Lago and Pérez-Lopéz have tried to narrow the range of uncertainty. Growth rates calculated by Mesa-Lago and Pérez-Lopéz are, on average, less than half the size of the official Cuban statistics and seem on par with the rest of Latin America. Brundenius and Zimbalist disagree with Mesa-Lago and Pérez-Lopéz. They defend higher rates of growth for the Cuban economy, although their estimates are still lower than official figures.[11]

Even if we do not know exactly how much Cuba has grown since the revolution, it is fair to say that the 1960s were tough years. At best, real growth may have made up for the increase in population, if that, leaving per capita income constant. But in the early 1970s, growth picked up and with a little help from Soviet friends, the economy kept moving until the mid-1980s. After 1986, one bad year followed another.

**How Rich Is Cuba?**

Zimbalist and Brundenius (1989) calculated that Cuban GDP per capita in 1985 was somewhere between $3,245 and $3,756 (in 1980 dollars). This estimate would put Cuban per capita income above that of any other Latin American country, including Venezuela. Other Cubanologists, however, would not hesitate to divide this estimate by two.

Table 2.2 shows the per capita income of seven Latin American countries between 1979 and 1989. This data indicate that Cuba's average income is higher than that of Peru's and lower than Chile's average income, suggesting that Cuba is not among the richest Latin American Countries. Table A.3 in the statistical appendix offers different estimates for comparison.

**Table 2.2**
GNP per capita, U.S. dollars,* selected countries, 1979–1989

|            | 1979  | 1989  |
|------------|-------|-------|
| Argentina  | 2,230 | 2,160 |
| Brazil     | 1,780 | 2,540 |
| Chile      | 1,690 | 1,770 |
| Costa Rica | 1,820 | 1,780 |
| Mexico     | 1,640 | 2,010 |
| Peru       | 730   | 1,010 |
| Cuba (WB)  | 1,410 |       |
| (Tabares)  | 1,817 | 1,837 |

* The World Bank calculates GNP per capita using a conversion factor that, for *any* year, is the average of the exchange rate for that year and the exchange rates for the two preceding years, after adjusting them for differences in relative inflation between the country and the United States. An alternative conversion factor is used when the official exchange rate is judged to diverge by an exceptionally large margin from the rate effectively applied to foreign transactions.

Sources: World Bank, *World Development Report 1981, 1990,* and *1991,* New York: Oxford University Press, 1981, 1990, and 1991; and Lourdes Tabares Neyra and Vilma Hidalgo de los Santos, "Una estimación de los principales agregados macroeconómicos de Cuba," Facultad de Economía, Universidad de la Habana, unpublished manuscript, Dec. 1990.

## Soviet Aid

By 1989 Cuba was as dependent on the Soviet Union as it had been on the United States thirty years before. Despite the downward trend of sugar's share in total exports, sugar still accounted for three quarters of export revenues. Until 1990, Soviet aid came in direct balance-of-payments and project aid as well as in price subsidies for sugar, nickel, petroleum, and other products. The Soviet payment on Cuban exports, compared to world prices, yielded the equivalent of $40 billion in grants between 1961 and 1988. Another $18 billion came in the form of concessional loans and development aid.[12]

Cuban officials once denied the significance of Soviet aid; the new take on this issue is that aid barely made up for the negative consequences of the U.S. embargo. Table 2.3 shows an estimate of Soviet aid to Cuba. During the last ten years it has exceeded 11 percent of Cuban gross social product.

Estimates of Soviet aid depend on how one converts rubles to dollars, the comparable world prices one attaches to barter deals, and how one handles services like transportation. The CIA estimates that in 1989 Cuba received $4.5 billion in export subsidies and $1.4 billion in other development aid from the Soviet Union. In 1990, the Soviets cut their aid to $2.2 billion in subsidies. Trade credits and development assistance, including help in the construction of two nuclear power plants, amounted to $1.3 billion in 1990.

While the level of Soviet aid is hotly debated, the cut in aid and trade relations that began in 1990 has already forced the economy into an undeniable economic crisis. By September 1991, the Soviets were pulling out troops from Cuba and asking the West to include sugar in its food aid to the Soviet Union. Cuba was preparing for the "zero option" in case all subsidized trade with the Soviet Union dries up. East European supplies of butter, buses, medicines, grains, and fertil-

**Table 2.3**
Soviet aid to Cuba, 1977–1989 (percent of GSP)

| Period | Soviet subsidy for Cuban sugar | Soviet subsidy for Cuban trade deficit | Total |
|---|---|---|---|
| 1978–1980 | 9 | 1 | 10 |
| 1981–1983 | 8 | 2 | 10 |
| 1984–1986 | 11 | 4 | 15 |
| 1987–1989 | 12 | | |

Note: The difference between Soviet and world market prices for sugar is the conventional measure of Soviet sugar subsidies to Cuba. Because little sugar is actually traded in the "world market," the table uses the price Cuba might have received from key market-economy partners. Between 1987 and 1989, estimates of the sugar subsidies' share in GSP vary between 11 percent and 17 percent, depending on the source one uses for total product.
Sources: Jorge Domínguez, *To Make a World Safe for Revolution*, Cambridge: Harvard University Press, 1989, Table 4.2, p.87; and CEPAL, *Estudio económico de América Latina y el Caribe, 1989, Cuba*, United Nations, Nov. 1990.

izer have almost come to a complete standstill. Cuban trade fell approximately 25 percent during the first half of 1991, compared to the first half of 1990.[13]

Scholars have tried to figure out whether Castro was a Marxist-Leninist from the start or whether he was simply switching gears in response to the economic incentive of attracting Soviet aid. Some question his ideology, but no one doubts his nationalism. Might an extreme economic shock lead Castro to change his colors?

## Social Progress

In the past thirty years, Cuba has made impressive gains in social welfare. Illiteracy and infant mortality rates are the lowest in Latin America. Thanks to an excellent and broadly accessible health care system, Cuban life expectancy is seventy-five years. (Life expectancy is seventy-six years in the United States and sixty-nine years in Mexico.) Less easily quantified, but apparent to any visitor, are achievements in racial integration and women's rights. The state provides daycare for working mothers. Blacks are well represented among the elite scientists in biotechnology, and groups of friends on casual outings are racially mixed. Moreover, there is an absence of extreme malnutrition in the streets of Havana. Gains in basic welfare have clearly benefited a wide spectrum of the population.

There are two ways to look at these achievements. The first view emphasizes that Cuba ranks at the top of Latin American countries on many social welfare indicators (table 2.4). Cubans enjoy better health and education than Bolivians and Hondurans. Despite a lower average income, Cubans also enjoy longer lives and lower childhood mortality than Brazilians. Moreover, aggregate data often masks the presence of groups with extremely high rates of illiteracy and infant mortality where income distribution is unequal. The failure of many Latin American governments to direct resources toward meeting the basic needs of the poor is woefully apparent, while the Castro regime has maintained a laudable commitment to educating and feeding all Cubans.

The second perspective says that Cuba is not alone in its progress on social welfare. Compared to other countries in the Caribbean basin, such as Barbados, Jamaica, Bermuda, Martinique, and Guadeloupe, Cuba's record does not distinguish itself. Jamaica entered the 1960s with similar indicators in life expectancy, literacy, and child mortality, and can now boast comparable progress. Data on basic indicators in Cuba in 1960 were reportedly biased by oversampling in urban areas. The same was probably true in Jamaica, which had roughly the same level of urbanization.

**Table 2.4**
Basic social indicators, Latin America and the Caribbean, selected
countries, late 1980s (except where indicated)

|  | Infant mortality (per thousand live births) | Adult illiteracy (percent of adults) | Income share of richest 20 percent of population as a multiple of the share of poorest 20 percent |
|---|---|---|---|
| Cuba | 12 | 4.0 | 3 |
| Barbados | 12 | 0.7 | |
| Costa Rica | 18 | 6.4 | 16 |
| Jamaica | 18 | 3.9 | 9 |
| Chile | 20 | 5.6 | 14* |
| Trinidad & Tobago | 20 | 3.9 | |
| Panama | 23 | 11.8 | 24* |
| Uruguay | 27 | 4.6 | 13* |
| Argentina | 32 | 4.5 | 7* |
| Venezuela | 36 | 13.1 | 11 |
| Mexico | 47 | 9.7 | 16* |
| Brazil | 63 | 22.3 | 26 |
| Honduras | 69 | 40.5 | 21* |
| Peru | 88 | 13.0 | 12 |
| Bolivia | 110 | 25.8 | |
| Haiti | 117 | 62.4 | |

*mid-1970s.
Source: Inter-American Development Bank, *Economic and Social Progress in Latin America*, 1990; World Bank *World Development Report 1990*, and *1991*; United Nations, *Human Development Report 1990*; Jacques Lecaillon et al., *Income Distribution and Economic Development: An Analytical Survey*, Geneva: International Labor Office, 1984; Andrew Zimbalist and Claes Brundenius, *The Cuban Economy*, Baltimore: Johns Hopkins University Press, 1989.

Table 2.5 shows the progress achieved over approximately twenty-five years in five countries. The Dominican Republic is often presented as the misbehaving capitalist counter-example to the Cuban model. Despite the two countries' similar reliance on sugar exports, the Dominican Republic was much poorer than Cuba thirty years ago, and that continues to be true today.

Chile and Costa Rica have made even more impressive gains than Cuba in reducing child mortality. Costa Rica and Chile may have been able to achieve more than most Latin American countries because neither has had the long-standing class and racial divisions common to other countries in the region. For Cuba to overcome the backwardness that prevailed at the time of the revolution, a massive shift in political power toward agricultural workers was required. Thus revolution may have been necessary.

To ask what would have happened in Cuba in the absence of socialism is to pose a question that is too hypothetical to answer convincingly. No two countries are the same. Jamaica did not have Batista, and it did benefit from some aspects of British colonization. Cuba might have achieved even more had it not felt the need to spend so much money on defense: the ratio of military to health and education expenditures in Cuba is four times that of Jamaica (and 60 percent higher than that in Chile and the Dominican Republic). But high military expenditures were also part of the deal that kept relations with the Soviets good and made economic growth possible.

Costa Rica has received almost as much foreign aid as Cuba and has been successful in promoting equality, growth, and democracy. This example challenges assertions that progress in social welfare in developing countries can only be achieved as a result of socialist revolution. Although both Chile and Jamaica went through short episodes of socialism, few people would claim that these were the principal years in which gains

**Table 2.5**
Trends in welfare indicators, selected countries, 1960–1988

|  | Cuba | Jamaica | Dominican Republic | Chile | Costa Rica |
|---|---|---|---|---|---|
| Life expectancy |  |  |  |  |  |
| 1960 | 63 | 63 | 52 | 57 | 62 |
| 1987 | 75 | 73 | 67 | 72 | 75 |
| Under age five child mortality |  |  |  |  |  |
| 1960 | 87 | 88 | 200 | 142 | 121 |
| 1988 | 14 | 21 | 80 | 27 | 22 |
| Literacy rate |  |  |  |  |  |
| 1970 | 87 | 97 | 67 | 89 | 88 |
| 1985 | 92 | 98 | 78 | 92 | 92 |
| Percent of labor in agriculture |  |  |  |  |  |
| 1965 | 33 | 37 | 59 | 27 | 47 |
| 1985–87 | 24 | 25 | 46 | 20 | 28 |

Source: United Nations, *Human Development Report 1991*, New York: Oxford University Press, 1991.

occurred. Certainly central planning was not an element in these success stories. But the lingering presence of leftist ideas and international pressure may have prevented laissez-faire regimes from ignoring the poor.

In moving forward, central planning and socialism will prove to be the wrong tools for maintaining Cuba's high level of social welfare. The hardships of maintaining socialism, in the absence of Soviet cooperation and in the face of U.S. opposition, may well translate into a deterioration in basic indicators. The Castro regime has promised that Cubans will have a guaranteed income to meet their needs in the current crisis. As resources dry up, the promise will be hard to keep.

# 3    Impressions

The world is changing, Moscow is changing, and so is the Moscow-Havana relationship. For the sake of world revolution, Castro sent his troops to Africa, and the Soviets paid the bill. As the Soviets cut military expenses, Cuban troops returned home. In 1991 Cuba was still a base for Soviet ships and electronic espionage, but not for long. With Soviet disintegration and the U.S.-Soviet honeymoon, Cuba's strategic value to the Soviets disappeared.

For more than a year, Moscow quietly put up with sneers from Fidel Castro about the folly of the changes under way in the Soviet Union. But by early 1990, the Soviet press launched a volley of blasting scorn toward the Cuban leader. It depicted Cuba as an impoverished police state still mimicking Brezhnev-era communism.[1] The Soviet press reflected a growing ideological division between the countries and presaged the cutbacks in aid and loans, which were viewed in Moscow as a drag on the budget.

As a consequence, Fidel Castro's revolution has been beset by shortages. The decline in Soviet trade forced Cuba into an extreme form of economic adjustment, worse than that faced by other Latin American countries after the debt crisis. Cuba's lack of international competitiveness and the dominance of sugar in the economy makes adjustment difficult. Most countries protect their sugar producers; finding buyers to replace the Soviets will be difficult. By 1991 the Cuban economy was undergoing a deep crisis, which required drastic measures to cut the use of energy and materials. Factories were shut down and 750,000 Chinese bicycles were on order to replace cars and buses. Workers who lost their jobs were sent to farm camps, to work alongside bureaucrats drafted to contribute two weeks of manual labor.

In June 1991, we decided to assess what was going on by looking at the country firsthand. Because Treasury Department regulations effectively ban leisure and business travel to Cuba, Americans wishing to visit Cuba must bend or break the law by traveling through Canada, unless they are scholars, journalists, or Cuban-Americans visiting relatives on the island. As scholars, we seized the opportunity to join a research group that is working with Cuban economists.

## A Trip to Cuba

That Cubans crave Western goods was evident the moment we walked into the airline terminal in Miami. Hundreds of Cubans visiting or returning home to Havana were lined up with enormous duffel bags. Gaudy women's hats seemed to portend a bad national aesthetic, until a closer look showed dozens of barrettes and ponytail holders neatly pinned on the hat ribbons. No one pretends to fool Cuban customs agents, who evidently look the other way.

The thirty-minute flight to Havana with Haiti Trans-Air departs at 10:30 a.m., but at 6:30 a.m. we were already standing in a long line. Like most people in front of us, we did not know whether Cuba had approved our visa and whether we would be able to depart. We did. The plane was packed.

On arrival, one rediscovers the cars of childhood: De Sotos, Kaisers, big Buicks from the 1950s, assorted Chevrolets, and Packards roll along. Cubalse, an agency that provides services for foreigners, claims there are about 60,000 pre-1959 autos still operating in Cuba. Some of the "classics" are lined up for sale in an aircraft hangar. Prices range from $4,500 to $25,000, shipping and repair costs not included.

Decaying cars and hotels testify to the vanished American presence. It did not take long to find out that hotels are divided into two groups: the old and the new. In the old hotels, such as El Presidente, dowdiness is the order of the day: elevators creep, telephone lines crackle, carpets have big stains, and water drips rather than gushes from faucets. At the new hotels, such as The Plaza in Havana and Sol Palmeras in Varadero (a beach resort three hours by car from Havana), the accommodations look like mid-priced to upscale hotels elsewhere in the Caribbean. New televisions and chic decor reflect the influence of foreign firms, who built these hotels as joint ventures with the Cuban government during the late 1980s.

For years Cuba excelled in social tourism. It offered tours of model communes and sugar plantations to display the victories of socialism to sympathetic Westerners. In recent years, however, the need to generate hard currency has brought in hedonism in place of social tourism. Jets now unload increasing numbers of Canadians, Germans, and Italians who immediately head to Varadero, the center of Cuba's effort to develop tourism. The beach at Varadero is spectacular. But the common tourist perks are still missing: direct international calls cannot be made, and souvenirs range from cigars and portraits of Che Guevara to more expensive cigars. The isolation of the beach resorts, combined with the prohibition against small private shops and restaurants, creates a sterile atmosphere. Tourism earned Cuba $250 million in 1990, but it has not been able to shore up a weak economy. And it will not until Americans can go to Cuba.

Havana's boulevards were pleasantly quiet, thanks to the lack of gasoline. Stories circulating in the United States about donkey carts delivering goods were in fact too optimistic; the country lacks fodder necessary to shift completely to animal power. Worse, there were few goods to deliver.

Most goods were rationed. Food shops portioned out small allotments of rice and milk. Long lines formed outside bakeries, as families waited for their daily loaf of bread. Making bread at home to avoid the wait was not an alternative: there was no flour to buy. One woman said she used to enjoy baking cakes with her children, but could not get the flour anymore. Even fabric consumption was limited to four meters per person per year. Anyone wearing relatively new clothing inevitably admitted that they managed to get it from abroad. Cuban women were still allowed a choice of one bra or two panties per year, but not both, and only in the size available at the moment. A variety store had no more than a dozen goods for sale, among them five rubber gaskets, three pieces of pipe, a stack of bottle brushes, and ugly plastic flowers. Were these goods the leftover dregs from a more prosperous era? Or did some bureaucrat decide that plastic flowers were a high priority? Women clearly wanted lipstick and nail polish. A hotel elevator operator proudly revealed a new lipstick bought in the United States by a cousin. Women seemed ready to replace revolutionary consciousness with mercenary spirit.

Old Havana was especially depressed. Little is left of the splendor of pre-revolutionary days. As there is no paint to buy, buildings are flaking and peeling; once-stately homes are falling into ruin. In preparation for the Pan-American Games, a few buildings on the waterfront were getting a coat of shocking pink and purple paint. The rest of the old city is depressingly gray. Many verandas like those in New Orleans lack signs of life that might be easily encouraged with a contest to promote colorful porch gardens. The streets are littered. Some would say this is because labor is expensive; others would say it reflects a fundamental lack of concern about the quality of life.

For a country with roughly the population of Chile and far less land, the capital city is strangely quiet. Buses run, but far fewer than in Santiago or Kingston. People are not rushing around Havana's streets. They are standing in line for rations or hanging out. In some cases they stand in line to hang out.

Two lines serve people who want a little entertainment: the ice cream line and the hamburger line. After waiting half an hour for an ice cream at the famous Copelia, we passed our tickets to a grandfather in line with his daughter and granddaughter. "McCastro," the hamburger shop, serves soda and simple hamburgers. Customers in line said the burgers were so-so—not exactly inedible, but not worth the one-hour wait. Young kids did not mind the price of U.S. $2, which signals that there is too much money relative to goods and that the official exchange rate for the peso does not reflect its value.

Why wait so long for insipid food? Hunger was not the main motivation. It was still too early for the Brazilian soap opera on television, so there was nothing else to do. No one objected to the insanely inefficient service. When people reached the head of the line, they sat on a stool and lingered over their food, ignoring the line immediately behind them.

As tourists, we had access to plenty of food in the hotels. The catch is that everything had to be paid for in dollars. Still, at least in Havana and the surrounding area, there was no indication that people were hungry—yet.

People were well intentioned and congenial, even to Americans viewed as the root of their problems. Hotel service is as slow as anywhere else in Latin America. Construction workers hammer along at a pace adapted to the oppressive heat. Mechanics at the car rental agency keep things humming despite shortages of replacement parts. That the country works at all, in the face of demoralizing shortages, is astounding. There are widespread complaints that Cubans do not work hard enough. But there are no incentives to employ when the pressure hits, for example, at harvest time.

There are no street vendors or hawkers to remind us that we are in Latin America. Unlike Mexico, where employees of the state-owned telephone company used to drive taxis in their "off" hours, Cubans cannot easily set up a small business on the side. People say there are hairdressers and seamstresses, but few hang up a sign for services. A broken pipe meant waiting a few weeks for the state plumber to arrive. Access to most goods is too limited and the penalties too high for people to set up illegal shops and kiosks. The state not only fails to provide goods but prohibits people from filling the gap with informal markets.

In recent years, the black market for goods unavailable in state stores has expanded. Black market supplies come from visiting relatives and from technicians and East-bloc embassy workers with access to special stores reserved for foreigners. This merchandise has been resold to Cubans at five to six times its original price.

Looking across Havana's bay toward Florida, it was easy to see why enterprising Cubans launch rafts. Some of the shortages run against the grain. Why are people not raising vegetables in home gardens? Or transforming some of the country's abundant sugar into treats that can compete with Copelia? Although emigration is illegal and anyone caught trying to leave the country faces imprisonment, the land of opportunity beckons. According to the *New York Times* (July 16, 1991), 1,200 Cubans arrived by boat in Florida in the first half of 1991.[2] By August U.S. officials stopped accepting visa applications because it was flooded with more than it could possibly process that year.

Kids in school scamper about with plenty of freedom. The educational system is not a factory designed to make every student a high tech-whiz, but at least the kids seemed happy. Literacy remains a high priority. Despite the economic crisis, schools have composition paper and pencils. Daycare centers continue to have access to food, ensuring that children get at least minimal nutrition. The daycare center we visited also emphasized personal hygiene, with a toothbrush for each child lined up under his name. The system has not generated the underclass of kids condemned to beg, steal, and pick through garbage that one finds elsewhere in Latin America.

Older women proudly talk about their children's successes. Compared to other developing countries, a high proportion of Cubans are trained as doctors, scientists, and technicians. But not all are able to use their skills. One engineer in a hospital-bed factory said the shop was not producing because of a lack of materials. Residents in Havana balked at the prospect of farm labor, required by the state as a means of facing the economic crisis.

Biotechnology workers form an elite group and enjoy special privileges. The schools where they are trained are highly competitive: only 4 percent of applicants were accepted to the preparatory high school program in 1984–85. Advanced training in microbiology is obtained abroad. The state has invested heavily to get biotechnology exports off the ground. A modern facility boasts some of the best equipment in the world, much of it made by LKB/Pharmacia of Sweden and JEOL of

Japan; the equipment is used to produce vaccines and drugs for export. The latest issues of *The Journal of Electron Microscopy* were lying open on laboratory benchs.

Outside the field of biotechnology, higher education is less impressive. The best technical bookstore in the country held only a few hundred volumes, many containing reprinted speeches of Che and Castro. The medical shelf held a few chemistry books and one book on the treatment of burns. Economic books described Cuba's sugar industry, but none presented theories on how international markets work. This absence is costly, given the country's need to master global market mechanisms no matter how extensively the domestic economy is planned.

## Any Dissent?

Within Cuba, opinions about the island's economic and ideological isolation vary from growing discontent to nationalistic support for state policies. Castro uses anti-imperialist rhetoric to rally crowds. In public, government officials deny that Cuba is in crisis. After all, crisis is a capitalist concept. What they are suffering from is euphemistically named a "special period".

Professors of economics at the University of La Havana go along with the official line. They do not teach how markets work, even oligopolistic global markets that control Cuba's future in biotechnology. They condemn Cuba's experiment with peasant markets because a few poor farmers got rich, and do not acknowledge the peasant markets' positive impact on increased food supplies. Socialism is the religion that offers solutions. The director of graduate studies at the University of La Havana told us, "socialism is scientific. It is the truth. And the Cubans shall not forsake principles." Another said that under socialism, she has inner calm and is at peace with herself: "I like to have my life and that of my kids assured and protected. It is safer to live in socialist Cuba than in the United States." They agree with Castro's complaints about the difficulty of building up communism when others slander socialism, destroy its values, discredit its party, and chip away at social discipline. Their rhetoric and posturing—understandable coming from party hacks—is inexcusable from those who must help the next generation find its way in a vastly different world. In response to questions about Cuba's options, academics proudly repeated Fidel Castro's ubiquitous slogan "Socialism or Death." Cubans joke that "Socialism or Death" does not stand for real choice, because socialism and death are the same thing.

The economists who hosted our trip were more eager to find solutions to Cuba's economic woes. Most were trying to figure out the prospects for expanding tourism, increasing access to the Middle East's sugar market, or reducing Cuban imports. Yet none were exploring the possibility of a shift toward a market economy. One claimed to be a socialist, but "pragmatic." With Castro's antimarket rhetoric, pragmatic intellectuals do not dare to be anything but socialists. The result is that good economists cannot seriously study Cuba's options for the future.[3]

Unless Cubans can discuss the merits and pitfalls of capitalism, they will not be able to avoid its worst aspects when it arrives. With no grounding in policies to address problems of inflation, unemployment, monopolistic pricing, environmental regulation, or bank failures, Cubans are unprepared for a rapid economic transition. When change comes, this knowledge vacuum may invite a grab for power among exiles.

Economic hardships and asphyxiating controls have eroded support for the communist regime. Cuban intellectuals and human rights campaigners have begun to denounce one-party rule. A group of ten Cuban intellectuals, most of whom belong to the nation's official writers and artists' union, signed a statement calling for a return to free markets for farmers, amnesty for prisoners of conscience, and national debate. The official Communist Party newspaper, *Granma*, denounced the writers as obscure drunkards and partners in a CIA-sponsored destabilization plot.

While having a drink at *La Bodeguita del Medio*, we talked to an artist who strongly criticized socialism as the "sharing of poverty" and accused the government of corruption. His example may be a sign of broader dissatisfaction, but there is no organized revolt. People we interviewed on the street said opposition groups have no shortage of leadership, but they declined to give names. A few weeks later, the government arrested activists suspected of planning protests for the Pan-American Games.

Soldiers on the street look relaxed, but they are quick to stop activities that undermine the state's control. In November 1991, vendors accused of selling rum, cigarettes, food, and soap were arrested and instantly tried at night, a few meters from the scene of their crimes in a canteen intended for construction workers. *Granma* reported that the trials were "exemplary." In the United States, reports circulate about the abuse of electroshock therapy and psychiatric drugs to silence opposition leaders. Amnesty International and Americas Watch have called for pressure on the Cuban government to respect human rights, a goal many Cubans dismiss as unattainable in the face of U.S. threats.

### Blinders from the Past

American traveling companions, once avid fans of Cuban socialism, kept reminding us that things were better a few years ago. The data support this: the 1989 level of Cuban total product was the same as in 1984,[4] and the economy continued to deteriorate in 1990 and 1991, implying a higher income per capita in 1984 than now. Fewer goods were rationed in the past, and variety stores most likely had something to sell. But exactly how much better things were is hard to gauge. Clearly, the buildings have been crumbling for years, clothes are worn out, and cars have been kept alive out of necessity, not out of sentimentality.

Cuba has been the darling of progressives in the United States, and its impressive gains in social welfare have been held up as an example to the rest of Latin America, where elites would rather shoot the poor than feed them. But few U.S. leftists have supported the Soviet Union: Stalin's repression brought about a dramatic split in the U.S. Communist Party in the 1940s, with most leftists agreeing that the USSR was not a utopia. In promoting Cuba as an example of successful development, many denied the importance of Soviet aid.

The Council for Mutual Economic Assistance (Comecon), the economic trading unit comprised of the East European bloc and the Soviet Union, represented more than 87 percent of total Cuban trade in 1988. In the first half of the 1980s, Cuba benefited from privileged access to the markets for sugar, nickel, and citrus fruit in socialist countries. During that period, Cuba also benefited from prices higher than those prevailing in the world market for its exports, compensatory mechanisms for import price increases, preferential long-term credits, preferential rates for technical assistance, and fuel reexports in convertible currency. After 1986, sugar prices went down, profits on reexported oil declined, and the weather did not help crops. Since 1989, Comecon countries have backed away from Cuba: Poland reneged on a deal for Cuban citrus and is instead buying from Southern Europe and Israel. Hungary is demanding hard currency payment for bus parts. Czechoslovakia has recalled technical experts.

During 1990, trade with Eastern Europe practically disappeared as Cuban imports from this area fell by 26 percent in relation to 1989; imports from the Soviet Union fell by 11 percent. The decline in trade volume is at least as important as the decline in price subsidies. At the end of the first quarter of 1991, none of the agreed exports from the Soviet Union had arrived in Cuba, except for fuel.[5]

Although shortages are glaringly obvious, official commentary on the current crisis is conditioned by the government's past refusal to acknowledge the significance of Soviet aid. Visitors' references to Soviet aid are repeatedly corrected as "mutual cooperation." The Soviets did indeed benefit strategically from their ties with Cuba, thus it is hard to quibble with the correction. But getting the Cubans to acknowledge the profound importance of Soviet economic links to the Cuban economy is difficult. By extension, Cuban officials are also hesitant to discuss food shortages and the lack of basic goods apparent on the streets of Havana.

Like a rich dowager who has lost her fortune, Castro threw one last big party, the Pan-American Games, in August 1991. Officials admitted that, had they anticipated the current economic crisis, they would not have agreed to host the games five years earlier. Pride prevented them from canceling the games, or even minimizing the scope of preparations. Twenty-seven new sports-related buildings, including a vast stadium on the outskirts of Havana, and 1,400 apartments were put up in a frantic effort to host the games in style. According to one estimate, the construction cost $500 million. The 8,000 workers who toiled twelve-hour days to finish the job went home to showers without soap. The games were a smashing success:

stro does recognize that certain changes must take place.
he knows that market economics and open politics may
off the chain reaction observed in Eastern Europe and
aragua. He resists them, and promotes enclave sectors
h as tourism and biotechnology. Is there a painless solu-
to the Cuban economic crisis? Patchwork will not do the

he loss of trade relations with the Soviet Union and East-
Europe represents a critical blow to the Cuban economy.
the face of the U.S. embargo, alternative markets offer
ited and insecure choices. Convincing the United States to
sanctions would prove no panacea, for access to the U.S.
gar market requires special quotas. But a normalization of
ations would bring American tourists and open doors for
her exports.

Socialist rhetoric prevails: it charges through Castro's
eeches and rolls across every billboard in the country. The
etoric adds to Cuba's isolation by perpetuating hostile
lations with the United States. A country that imports
early all of its oil, most of its food, and the few luxuries that
xist cannot afford to cut itself off. Small doses of foreign
vestment will not make up for the need to gain access to new
arkets now that the East bloc has collapsed.

Nor can limited ventures with foreign firms replace well-
unctioning markets and overcome the rigidities of central
lanning. Under capitalism, the financial system provides
incentives to owners of capital to invest and hire labor, and
prices work as signals of scarcity to producers and consumers.
Distributional equity is not assured in the absence of government intervention, but the system is flexible in response to
shortages. Cuba's current strategy tries to harness profit-
seeking firms while repressing local entrepreneurs. The result
is that Sprite can be found in all major hotels, but vegetables

Cuban athletes won one medal after ar
system as the source of their success.

The morning after, reality had not cha
meat, no paper, and no gasoline. Indeed
Pan-American Games, a coup attempt
portended the collapse of Cuba's most i
must realize that its past achievements o
the future. Under new global conditions, ;
is far from secure.

## Minor Adjustments to a Major Crisis

The government is desperately trying to p
the current crisis, referring to it as a "spec;
of peace." It frankly tells Cubans that they
ships in the coming years as a result of chanξ
the Soviets. Yet it also insists that solutions
through aggressive promotion of tourism ;
ment of biotechnology products. The plan i
and boost food production and activities th

Cuban leaders point to recent successes in
including the marketing of a hepatitis vaccine
trade with Latin America as signs that the C
could revive. Recovery will be a tough job. T
ill-equipped to compete internationally. Prodι
is geared toward sugar, a product that the new
in Latin America will not buy. Cuban biotechnι
its setbacks, with complaints of patent theft aι
vaccines. Tourism is not without drawbacks.
capitalist countries spread ideological contami
also undermine a xenophobia that sustains suμ
Castro regime. Most tourists stay in isolated rε
they must pay their hotel and restaurant bills v
which Cubans do not have. Cubans bitterly resε

are scarce. Cuba needs small domestic producers for sound economic growth.

Cuba needs shock therapy—a speedy shift to free markets. *El que no cambia todo, no cambia nada.* Lingering over a "third way," some hybrid of socialism and capitalism, will not ease Cuban entry into the world economy. We address the limitations of this approach in the next chapter. To seize new opportunities, people must be healthy and educated. Here Cuba has an advantage, which it must not lose by letting the crisis linger on and erode the resources needed for health and education.

# 4    Prospects for the Future

In the early 1990s, Florida's governor created a commission to study the potential effects of Cuba's democratization on his state. Cuban-Americans began to plan a new constitution for the island. About the same time, at a meeting in Chile of the Christian Democratic Organization of America, Costa Rica's former president Oscar Arias and thirty Latin American politicians expressed optimism about the rise of democracy in Cuba. Castro showed no signs of acceding to their calls for change. Who will overthrow Castro? The most likely scenario is a military coup. But with General Arnaldo Ochoa's trial for drug trafficking, Castro tightened his control, strengthened the secret police, and purged the party and the military. Apparently there is no one left among the Cuban military who is willing and powerful enough to pull off a coup. Getting rid of an obstinate dictator is difficult, even when he does not have legitimacy, as in Noriega's case. Castro's extraordinary political resilience should not be underestimated.

Despite growing economic distress, the sixty-three-year-old Comandante remains popular. Most Cubans believe that Cuba's problems are not Castro's fault. Instead they blame the political upheavals of Eastern Europe and the American embargo. Though frustrated by restrictions on individual freedoms, they seem prepared to wait for Castro's end before demanding radical change. Castro may hold onto power for quite some time.

Who will be in the driver's seat when Cuba changes? Cuban exiles? Repressive murderers like Pinochet? Establishing the political legitimacy of a transition to capitalism is tricky. The current regime still has a chance to influence what the transition looks like. Ironically, if Castro were willing, he could lead a transition to capitalism. As much as Cubans doubt the wisdom of his stubborn adherence to socialism, they respect his intelligence, shrewdness, and determination. His rhetoric, however, rules out any hope that he will seize the opportunity.

Nonetheless, current circumstances will force Castro to introduce "historically necessary reforms" to keep Cuba afloat. Joint ventures have already introduced limited autonomy in a few enterprises. Special privileges are also being used to prevent the defection of highly skilled workers, including biotechnology scientists and successful musicians like Los Van Van. In October 1991, trade artisans were given limited rights to sell their skills privately. Eventually, economic decentralization—or increasing hardship—will erode Castro's power. A shift to capitalism seems inevitable, though it may follow a period of decay and reform under socialism.

Cuba's centrally planned economy (characterized by state ownership, centralized decisionmaking, rigidly administered prices, heavy state subsidies, and an absence of markets) is reminiscent of Romania before Ceausescu's overthrow; without Soviet subsidies or access to the U.S. market, centralism cannot last in Cuba. Forced labor, unpaid overtime, and repression will not overcome Cuba's dependence on trade. Castro certainly wants to avoid Ceausescu's end. That means reforms will necessarily shape policies in the next few years.

## The Hybrid Way

One possible reform package would combine central planning and market mechanisms, changes toward enterprise autonomy, and the gradual introduction of market prices and profit incentives. Ideological barriers and an unchanged political and institutional framework hinder even this limited change. But if such a system is introduced, Cubans will soon realize, as the Hungarians did before them, that the old system cannot simply be improved. It must be revamped.

A hybrid model cannot work. It may sound like the path to a smoother transition, compared to a full-fledged shift to free markets. Bureaucrats may prefer this option, believing that it allows them to control the economy. But whom would such a system benefit? Not the ordinary Cuban worker, whose wage must remain low for the country to achieve any degree of international competitiveness. Nor will it benefit the extraordinary worker, with a willingness to hustle, for she will find that credit rationing, import controls, and bureaucracy stand in the way of setting up a small business.

A hybrid system yields the worst of both systems: little foreign investment because the state fiddles too freely with the rules of the game, and glaring inequities that are excused as necessary incentives to attract elusive capital. Latin America experimented with hybrid models throughout the 1950s and 1960s. The result was persistent poverty and corruption.

After three decades of isolation, Castro's advisers unwisely recommend the old import-substitution industrialization model, which prevailed in Latin America during the 1950s. That model, relying on heavy state intervention to overcome underdevelopment and propel growth, broke down for several reasons. Subsidies to industry put pressure on the budget, creating deficits that were financed with inflationary monetary growth. Firms with export potential had to buy inputs from inefficient domestic companies. Prices were used to redistribute income rather than allocate resources, creating bottlenecks in the supply of many goods. Cheap credit prevented industry from adopting labor-intensive technologies. Trade barriers stymied exports. A regulatory morass meant that economic decision-making was determined by political advantage: firms got greater returns from lobbying and catering to policymakers than from producing efficiently. The result was a system of patronage that allowed the government to extend economic favors in exchange for political allegiance. With guaranteed control of the domestic market, firms abused their monopolistic powers to charge prices far in excess of world levels.

Until recently in most Latin American countries, the state had its fingers in everything, from railroads and steel to communications. State-owned firms ran huge deficits that were financed by printing money. Price controls were applied to stop inflation, but led instead to speculative hoarding or to factory shutdowns. Few foreign firms found these countries attractive: they could not count on getting imported supplies through customs; tax rates were high and kept changing; the exchange rate was chronically overvalued; and labor was obstinate. Only in large countries blessed with extensive natural resources, such as Brazil, Mexico, and Argentina, could such bad policies persist without widespread misery. Latin Americans organized massive street protests, but it proved difficult to unseat a fifty-year streak of economic mismanagement.

Cuba is liable to run into the same problems with a hybrid model. Castro's joint ventures target tourism and exports, but this does not ensure efficiency and competitiveness. As the principal investor in these joint ventures, the government may wind up absorbing heavy losses. Firms are likely to be pressured to buy inputs from state-owned monopolistic suppliers when cheaper inputs are available from abroad. The joint ventures also put the government in a bind as it determines prices, wages, and exchange rates: the more policymakers try to use prices to redistribute income, the less effective prices are in allocating resources. As long as the government holds onto key sectors of the economy, such as energy and communications, it is under political pressure to keep prices low. Skirting this through two-tiered pricing systems and multiple exchange rates has proven a recipe for corruption. As Cuba invites more joint ventures, one has to ask whether extensive state involvement in production, even if it is in strategic sectors, is the most efficient way to promote growth and redistribute income.

Cuba not only lacks the natural resources of countries that weathered an era of import substitution industrialization, it also lacks their industrial base. The Dominican Republic might offer a more realistic comparison, although it has dawdled behind Cuba.

## The Dominican Republic Road

Would the Dominican Republic be a suitable model for Cuba? Policy errors and a poorly developed economy have produced erratic performance in the Dominican Republic. With exports concentrated in nickel and sugar, the Dominican Republic is sensitive to swings in world prices. Rather than dampening these fluctuations, government policy has tended to exacerbate them. State-owned sugar enterprises run chronic losses. A decline in the world price of sugar tends to increase public sector deficits, which are in turn financed by money creation. The result is rapid inflation and capital flight as residents send their savings to Miami.

Joaquín Belaguer, who has ruled off and on since 1965, works on the principle that government should have a high profile. Heavy government spending on public works (including roads, water supplies, housing, and airports) has supported construction booms. But because these projects require imported inputs, they contribute to balance-of-payments deficits and inflation. Less touted by politicians is the state-owned electricity company, which is blamed for nearly all of the island's economic problems. It typically provides Santo Domingo with no more than eight hours of electricity a day.

Local industry is protected with high tariffs or bans on imports. Since 1987, all imports need approval from the central bank. Industry cannot compete internationally and generates little employment. The exception is the success of industrial free zones that produce circuit boards, computer terminals, alarm systems, textiles, and footwear for export. These zones operate with low taxes and no import tariffs. While most of the economy stagnates, these areas boom. A dual system with industrial free zones has prevented Dominicans from reaping the rewards of integration into the world economy: they work for very low wages in the duty free sector, but then pay high prices to domestic firms that have a stranglehold on the local market through tariffs and import bans. Cuba's current attempt at creating enclaves of foreign entrepreneurship is similar: it sends profits abroad while it imposes upon workers the high cost of state production for the domestic market.

The government of the Dominican Republic has used protectionism to ensure the profits of local industrialists, but it let the real minimum wage plummet throughout the 1980s to maintain international competitiveness. The system leads to a highly skewed distribution of income. The poorest half of the population receives only 18.5 percent of national income. Low-income housing projects help to dampen protests, but in a system that refuses to impose taxes on the rich, the poor ultimately pay for their own housing via inflation. A mixed system is not a solution to Cuba's problems.

## The Capitalist Solution

Cuba will soon be pushed toward capitalism. The economy is too specialized and consequently too dependent on trade to insulate itself from global changes. Cubans are too well aware of the alternatives to passively accept an endless downhill slide. The sooner Cuba takes steps toward capitalism, the easier will be the transition and the more likely existing social values will shape capitalism in Cuba.

We think the shift to capitalism is inevitable. Will Cuban capitalism bring growth, stability, and some fairness? Embracing capitalism does not necessarily imply success, measured on any of these counts. The possibilities range from social and political degeneration to economic prosperity. We look at these possibilities before discussing what Cuba must do.

## Capitalist Degeneration

Capitalism can run amok in Cuba. One scenario would involve a coup, followed by massive repression, economic invasion by exiles, and a return to the inequality of the 1950s. The fall of Allende's socialist regime in 1973 taught us that social programs can be easily dismantled, and with enough repression, voices of despair can be silenced. Those who spoke out against the sharp decline in wages, the reversal of land reform, or the loss of voting rights disappeared forever.

Even if Cuba avoids this tragic outcome, capitalism could still arrive with empty hands. Indeed, Cuba could easily share many of the problems of Nicaragua and Haiti. Both economies are in a state of disarray. Their governments lack the ability to finance growth because they are unable to tax or borrow. Political chaos and a brittle economy prevent domestic and foreign investment. As a consequence, current standards of living in these two countries are the lowest in the hemisphere. Will Cuba join them? Cuba should avoid the fate of Nicaragua and Haiti.

## The Nicaraguan Road

In the 1980s under the Sandinistas, Nicaragua's economy spun out of control. Partly due to the cost of fighting the Contras, the government deficit soared to 30 percent of GDP in 1983 and stayed in the 15–25 percent range thereafter. The war drew scarce resources from the rest of the economy, exacerbated labor shortages, and diverted foreign exchange to purchase weapons. Desperate to gain political support, the Sandinistas continued to build schools and health clinics, although the Contras blew them up as fast as they were built. They also subsidized large agricultural exporters with a multiple exchange rate system and cheap credit. By 1988 inflation had reached 11,500 percent and output had fallen to levels of the late 1960s. Urban workers bore the brunt of the mess: real wages fell by more than 70 percent.

After ten years of fierce U.S. military and diplomatic efforts to destabilize the Sandinistas, Violeta Barrios de Chamorro, the anti-Sandinista candidate, won the presidential election on February 25, 1990. By the end of the year, the country continued to crumble under economic and political disarray, while the misery of the people had only increased. Prices rose 12,000 percent in 1990. Output fell 4.4 percent and seemed unlikely to fare much better in 1991. In March, 1991, unable to control inflation, the government tried fighting fire with fire and increased prices as part of a stabilization program. According to an informal estimate, Nicaraguans were shocked with price increases equivalent to an annual rate of 44,000 percent in the first three months of 1991. Privatization was slow to get off the ground because investors bargained hard over loss-making operations, and unions fiercely contested the transfers. Long gone are the literacy campaigns and health clinics that promised to bring rural Nicaraguans into the twentieth century.

A hard transition is gradually giving way to growth, thanks in part to aid and investments from abroad. The U.S. Agency for International Development came up with $241 million in 1990 and planned to disburse $219 million in 1991. Taiwan, Finland, and Sweden also offered aid or debt relief, and the World Bank began negotiations for a structural adjustment loan.[1] The clearing of Nicaragua's arrears of its debt to the World Bank and Inter-American Development Bank began in July 1990. By September 1991, President Chamorro's government was able to catch up on debt with credits from seventeen countries and a $193 million bridge loan from Colombia, Mexico, Spain, and Venezuela. In the summer of 1991, inflation stopped. (It actually registered a slight negative rate in July.) Nicaraguans who had moved to the United States during the 1980s began to return in their Cherokees and Broncos. These "Miami boys" and other small-scale entrepreneurs are investing in small grocery stores, Nintendo rental shops, bars, and farms. The economy is slowly coming alive.

Nicaragua still has plenty of problems. President Chamorro's main challenge is to knit a highly polarized society back together. Former Contras, now called Recontras, dislike Chamorro's attempt to pacify the Sandinistas by granting them control of the military. Political murders continue at an alarming rate. The country has regressed to violent struggles between *caudillos*, reminiscent of those that marked its history in the 1800s. Political violence is the single most important barrier to growth in Nicaragua.

Would free elections and capitalism create misfortune in Cuba? The prospects for aid and investment from the exile community are certainly better than in Nicaragua. The economic picture is at least as good in the long run. But the initial adjustment could be even worse. Although socialism in Cuba and Nicaragua depended on Soviet aid, the two countries differ in important respects. Nicaragua has a large rural population dependent on subsistence agriculture. Even many medium-sized farms grow food. Economic collapse has a centrifugal force in Nicaragua: people retreat to the countryside or take refuge across porous borders. By contrast, Cuba is highly urbanized, and rural areas offer little relief from shortages of food because of the dominance of sugar in agriculture. Urban riots may well erupt. The Haitian specter waits in the wings.

**Haiti**

Cubans need not look far to learn the consequences of political violence. The Duvalier family ruled and plundered Haiti for nearly thirty years before it was overthrown by popular unrest in 1986. Since then, political violence by former members of the dreaded Tonton Macoutes (thugs who served as Duvalier's secret police) and meddling by the military have disrupted democracy and devastated the economy. Although Haiti has long been among the poorest countries of the hemisphere, the last five years have put it in a class by itself. With the violent end to democratic reforms in 1987, private investors' confidence in Haiti, foreign aid, and tourism all plummeted. By 1990 Haitian income per person had returned to its level of 1960, a scant $360 per year. Efforts to reform the tax system, reduce the fiscal deficit, and stabilize prices have not made a dent. Despite Haiti's low-cost labor, its proximity to the United States, and unused quotas that grant Haitian sugar and textiles concessional access to the U.S. market, the country is unable to parlay these advantages into economic growth.

By early 1991, for the first time in several years, the economic prospects looked better. But starting from zero, with a legacy of corruption and inefficiency to overcome, President Jean-Bertrand Aristide's administration was extremely vulnerable. Following a violent coup in October, President Aristide flew to Venezuela, and President Bush suspended all U.S. economic and military assistance to the Haitian government. The country returned to hell. The Organization of American States demanded that Haiti reestablish constitutional rule, but for many Haitians the coup was swarming with complexities. President Aristide, fantastically popular among the poor masses, has generated fears among the tiny elite who accuse him of openly legitimizing the use of violence to settle scores. There is no hope for economic prosperity in a country torn by violence and wrenched by class and racial tensions.

Economic success requires political stability. Tourists and businesspeople do not like dashing among bullets. And few firms place bets on a country where the president is unlikely to survive another year in office. Cubans' strong ideological values make a peaceful transition to capitalism doubtful and put its initial success at risk. The return of conservative Cuban exiles could lead to violence as fanatic fringes of the right and left collide. The absence of political upheaval does not prevent bad policies, but it is an important ingredient for growth. With the right combination of good policies and foreign support, it can contribute to a bonanza.

**The Fast Track: Chile**

Pinochet created capitalism par excellence out of the ashes of Allende's attempt to pursue socialism. After a rough start in the 1970s and early 1980s, the economy grew at an average rate of 6.7 percent per year between 1984 and 1990, and inflation has remained at less than 20 percent. Can it be done again?

The errors of the 1970s are often mistakenly identified as key ingredients in the Chilean miracle. When Pinochet first took power, he implemented an ultraconservative experiment involving massive devaluation, exorbitant interest rates, and elimination of most price controls. He also broke the back of unions by massacring activists. The repression and hardline policies brought nothing. Growth averaged 1.8 percent between 1974 and 1983. Bankruptcies skyrocketed. Chile amassed a huge debt, and it was among the hardest hit when the debt crisis struck.

Economic and political survival required a move to more moderate policies. What did Chile do right? First, it liberalized trade. It overshot initially, by combining reduced tariffs with an overvalued exchange rate that hurt domestic producers. But beginning in 1984, a pragmatic exchange rate, more moderate interest rates, and selective government intervention supported a recovery driven by export growth and the revival of foreign investment. Having pulled the rug out from under farmers in the 1970s, the government reintroduced limited price supports and improved credit. Marketing assistance, like that used by the Asian newly industrialized countries (NICs), provided commercial farmers with knowledge about markets for grapes and other fruits, now ubiquitous in U.S. supermarkets. Low tariff rates and export taxes pushed firms to look outward. The government also updated the operation of ports and transportation networks.

Debt conversion swaps attracted foreign firms in mining, forestry, and financial services. Most activities in the public sector were returned to private hands. Privatization was originally designed to return companies seized by the Allende government to their deprived owners. By the late 1970s the controversial process expanded to divestiture of other state assets.[2] But the 1982–83 financial crisis, caused both by the international debt crisis and unsustainable interest and exchange rates, forced massive rescue operations and liquidations. Privatization came to a halt as the government took over failing banks. When privatization resumed, it included a program known as "popular capitalism," which gave taxpayers an option to buy shares in the state-held banks at favorable credit terms.

Chile's privatization of its national pension fund has produced remarkably little grumbling. The new funds replaced the bankrupt state-run pension and retirement system. Under the new system, private firms collect payments, manage funds, and supervise distributions. Pensions have markedly increased, and payments to the disabled and widows are more than twice their previous level.

Real wages remain low: as of 1989, they still had not returned to their peak level of 1981. However, unemployment fell from 20 percent in 1982 to 6 percent in 1990. Repression had ebbed considerably by 1987, enough so that it was possible to democratically oust the dictator. Although President Patricio Alwyn's government would like to close the book on a painful sixteen years, it is committed to maintaining market-oriented policies in an effort to finance vital social spending. The miracle yielded high growth but is weak in distribution. The challenge is to combine high growth with more equality.

### A Cuban Miracle?

Can Cuba pull off growth rates in excess of 4 percent per year by following noninterventionist, outward-oriented policies such as those prescribed by the Chilean model? Cubans are asking themselves this question as they send economists to study export promotion in Chile. Even if the threat of stagnation is real, high levels of education and technical experience offer some hope for avoiding extreme marginalization. What is realistic?

Cuba has a highly skilled labor force, beautiful coastal resources, and an ideal location to exploit, if it can restore economic relations with the United States. Yet it faces constraints that must be calculated into any realistic appraisal of Cuba's future.

Middle Eastern countries are an important new market for Cuban sugar. But East bloc countries have been distancing themselves from Cuba as a way of signaling their desire to earn U.S. support. A full-fledged shift to capitalism could buy goodwill in the United States and open doors to the U.S. sugar market, where the going price in the late 1980s was more than twice the world level. Although the United States might not take up the entire Cuban harvest, countries that shy away from trade with Cuba because of U.S. pressure would be more willing to buy Cuban sugar if relations with the United States improved.

Sugar is bound to dominate the economy for some time, but it is unlikely to be the basis of sustained rapid growth under any system, capitalist or socialist. Sugar prices are already in a secular decline as a result of higher yields in beet production and the use of corn syrup and artificial sweeteners. As the Soviet Union slides downward and its demand for sugar falls, the entry of Cuban sugar into world markets will further depress prices. Beet producers in the United States will vehemently oppose granting significant quotas to Cuba.

Tourism stands out for its undeveloped potential. Cuba has 800 miles of beaches. The waters are a pristine aqua and the sand is soft as silk. The Keys, including Cayo Largo, offer excellent scuba diving and snorkeling. The first round of investment under capitalism will almost certainly concentrate on hotels. The government's task will be to ensure that development does not ruin the very resources that attract tourists.

The tourist industry is not limited to hotels. Vacationers like nightlife, shops, and restaurants. A shift toward a market economy would allow the development of small enterprises aimed at entertaining tourists while they take a break from suntanning on the beach. The individual quirks of these outfits give a place character, even if they are tacky. Massive hotels in the middle of nowhere (the model now in place) are depressing. Small shops and restaurants make a place work, and they bring in valuable dollars.

Tourism is the most promising sector, but Cuba must compete with the rest of the Caribbean and Central America. Other islands, Mexico, Belize, and Costa Rica have aggressively expanded their tourist infrastructure, including new airports, roads, telephone lines, and national parks to support tourism. The competitors know what sells: they are in touch with current fashions, nightclubs, and cuisine. Air conditioners must run; pools cannot shut down for cleaning at high noon on a hot day; and waitresses need to smile even when faced with complaints. Long accustomed to serving Soviet bureaucrats, Cubans have a lot to learn in this business.

Nickel, tobacco, citrus, and biotechnology are touted as major sources of foreign exchange. At the time of the revolution, nickel amounted to only 4 percent of exports; even with new equipment, it will not be a big player in the future. Tobacco earned only about $140 million in 1990, less than 2 percent of Cuba's exports. Does biotechnology offer a way out?

Potential buyers in biotechnology are the drug companies, which form a tight oligopoly with few entrants. Cuba will find that one condition for playing ball with the United States is recognition of patents. Drug companies have the political clout to insist on this. They also have the research and development capacity to one-up most Cuban inventions by designing better versions of the same thing. Firms outside the industry will not venture into this oligopolistic lair.

Advertising and testing of a new drug typically costs pharmaceutical companies at least $150 million. Cubans have targeted the low end of the market, where standards for effectiveness are not as high. The vaccines they sold to Brazil are said to have had low rates of prevention; AIDS-testing kits are inexpensive, but also somewhat less accurate than those used in developed countries; and the usefulness of interferon, an anti-viral protein and a major biotech export, is constantly thrown into doubt.[3] The market for Cuban goods is the developing world. Burned by price controls, erratic exchange rates, and inconsistent regulation, drug companies are steering clear of it. Can one of the multinational drug companies be convinced to buy Cuba's La Playa plant?

Hope for a big influx of foreign capital is probably unrealistic. The potential for real growth lies in opening markets to allow smaller firms to fill gaps in production.

Large firms will snap up major state-owned enterprises, but rapid growth in a capitalist Cuba will depend on smaller firms that can serve domestic markets and develop new exports. Long lists of goods in short supply—from shoes to service stations to safety pins—provide some sense of the potential for expansion. Cuba will never be self-sufficient, but the import content of consumer goods is now more comparable to tiny Grenada than to Chile. Wrapped soap need not come from Indonesia, a can of Sprite from Holland, and a barrette from a Miami K-mart, as is now the case. Production and packaging for the domestic market will expand in the absence of state prohibitions.

The fast-growth capitalist scenario also calls for small scale investment in exports. Throughout the Caribbean, midsize firms have set up manufacturing operations in textiles, electronics, and footwear. Relatively small-scale investment in agriculture could also develop new exports of coffee, cut flowers, and vegetables.

Small-scale exports take time to develop: firms need to figure out where the markets are, establish contacts, and develop a reputation for reliable production. No miracle will eliminate the island's dependence on sugar overnight.

Cuban exiles will be important investors in a post-communist Cuba, particularly in small to midsize firms. There are one million Cuban-Americans in the United States. Although the median income of Cuban-Americans is above that of other Hispanic groups in the United States, it still lags behind the national median. Most lack fabulous wealth. They do not own major drug companies and hotel chains, but they have enough cash and business acumen to run a host of smaller firms. The most vocal Cuban exile groups are extremely conservative, but there is a chance that political conflicts could turn out to be manageable: 47 percent of Cuban-Americans voted Democratic in 1983, and many "yucas"—young, upwardly mobile Cuban-Americans—are liberals. Now called *gusanos* (worms), Cuban-Americans could provide essential breathing space.

Islanders themselves are the principal source of entrepreneurship that a market economy can tap. Microenterprises throughout Latin America provide transportation, clothing, shoes, toiletries, and food for local markets. Cubans lack capital, but the startup costs in these industries are small. The state now operates a modern fishing fleet that lacks access to gasoline. Cubans would have more fish to eat if individuals were allowed to sell the catch they bring in from their own boats. And they would spend fewer hours waiting for buses if vans were allowed to run. The brief opening of peasant markets in the late 1970s and early 1980s showed that eggs and vegetables appear in the market if people are allowed to earn a few pesos in profit.

Cuba will face stiff competition in entering world markets. Negotiation on the U.S.-Mexico Free Trade Pact gives Mexico the edge in selling manufactured goods to the United States. Its workforce is now fairly well educated, wages are low, and the political situation is stable.

Moreover, Cuban policymakers know discouragingly little about running a market economy. They have not been exposed to textbook models of supply and demand, much less the messier reality that prevails. There will be a lot of mistakes in regulatory barriers, fiscal mismanagement, and market interventions. On the other side, a hands-off approach can stymie growth: firms need decent infrastructure, including roads, sewerage, and environmental regulation. Overbuilding has botched the tourist industry in countless places. The country also needs a legal structure that prevents wholesale fraud and a banking system that operates efficiently. How much can the government do effectively?

Even if Castro wakes up tomorrow a born-again capitalist, growth will take off slowly. Contrary to popular belief, entrepreneurs do not jump at opportunities the minute they appear. It takes time for firms to feel confident about investing in a new environment. Their interdependence also means that they prefer to locate near other firms. Success breeds success; accelerating from a dead halt is tough. What can Cuba do?

# 5              What Cuba Can Do

The race is on between Eastern Europe and Latin America to reach the promised land of free markets, private enterprise, and prosperity. Except for Cuba, countries compete to show who is best at rejecting the past. In the wild swing of the pendulum, yesterday's truth is today's heresy. Yesterday, pervasive public control of the economy was thought to be essential to promote social progress, decentralize power, and keep out foreign domination. Today's recipe is just the reverse. Large public sectors entail inefficiency, corruption, and misallocation of resources. Joint ventures and foreign ownership, the sooner the better, will undo three decades of mistakes and lead to prosperity.

Cuba has proven that it is possible to centrally plan an economy to achieve social progress. Until the mid-1980s, Cuba stood as an example of growth with equality in Latin America, although this success was made possible thanks to Soviet financing. Once aid evaporated, central planning proved to be an extremely costly method of allocating resources.

## Why Socialism Will Not Work

Without optimism, endless anxieties would ruin our best days. To believe in our own resilience is to know that we will somehow survive tough times. But waiting for manna from heaven is sheer irrationality, and among policymakers it is downright irresponsibility.

Despite the disappearance of trade with the six East European countries and a dramatic reduction in Soviet subsidies, with more cuts on the way, Cuban policymakers believe that it will be possible to adjust to the crisis without changing systems. Indeed, several Cuban economic reports project a recovery in 1995 or 1996 based on expansion of tourism and biotechnology, sugar sales to the Middle East and China, and import substitution. Their failure to admit that Cuba faces an enduring crisis stifles discussion of alternative economic models.

Cuba is an extremely open economy that depends on imports of goods from petroleum to grains to machinery. Autarky is not a sustainable option. The size and structure of the Cuban economy severely constrain the potential to adjust to a loss of Soviet aid, particularly if U.S.-Cuba relations remain hostile. In the next three sections we look at what Cuba produces, the imports on which it depends, and its trade relations with the world. The next few years will be grim under any scenario. If these years mark a transition to a more diverse market economy, they can lay the groundwork for growth; prolonging socialism will merely erode Cuba's economic base.

**Beyond Sugar: What Cuba Produces**

Sugar comprises three quarters of Cuba's exports, but it accounts for just 4 percent of the gross social product. Indeed, agriculture as a whole only accounts for 15 percent of GSP, and 21 percent of total employment. Most Cubans work in industry, commerce, education, and construction (table 5.1). In addition to sugar, the agriculture produces citrus, rice, tobacco, corn, bananas, beans, and other crops. Cuban indus-

**Table 5.1**
Cuban product and employment by sector, 1989

|  | Global social product by sector (percent of total GSP) | Employment by sector (percent of total employment) |
| --- | --- | --- |
| Industry | 44.2 | 21.8 |
| Agriculture | 15.1 | 20.5 |
| Construction | 9.8 | 9.8 |
| Transport | 6.9 | 5.8 |
| Communications | 1.0 | 0.9 |
| Commerce | 22.2 | 11.2 |
| Education and culture |  | 12.5 |
| Health, sports, tourism |  | 6.9 |
| Other activities | .8 | 10.6 |

Source: CEPAL, *Estudio económico de América Latina y el Caribe 1989: Cuba,* Santiago, 1990.

try produces steel, iron rods, fishing boats, tires, stoves, refrigerators, buses, cane harvesters, cement, shoes, glass bottles, and more. Impressive?

A closer look shows an economy that has little capacity to absorb foreign exchange shocks: basic foods are imported and industry depends heavily on components and energy from abroad. The economy is neither so backward that subsistence agriculture makes people immune to economic progress and decline, nor is it so developed and diversified that domestic production can fill the gaps left by shortages of imports (tables 5.2 and 5.3).

Cuba does not grow wheat, a key staple. Among Latin American countries, Cuba is a significant producer of rice, but it must still import 50 percent of the rice it consumes. The feedgrain consumed by livestock is largely imported. Forty-four percent of Cuba's imports in 1989 were in the form of

**Table 5.2**
Composition of Cuban imports, 1989

|  | Imports (percent of total imports) |
|---|---|
| Combustible materials and related products | 32.4 |
| Machinery and transport equipment | 31.1 |
| Manufactured products | 13.7 |
| Food, live animals, beverages, and fats | 12.5 |
| Chemical products | 6.5 |
| Noncombustible raw materials | 3.8 |

Source: CEPAL, *Estudio económico de América Latina y el Caribe 1989: Cuba*, Santiago, 1990.

**Table 5.3**
Share of imported goods in Cuban domestic consumption, 1986–1989 (percent)

| Product | Imports divided by domestic production + imports – exports |
|---|---|
| Foodstuffs for animal consumption | 87 |
| Cereals for human consumption | 100 |
| Oils and fats | 98 |
| Butter without salt | 90 |
| Beans | 90 |
| Rice | 49 |
| Fertilizers (raw materials) | 94 |
| Pesticides and herbicides | 98 |
| Textiles, leather, soap, and perfumes | 90–100 |
| Cans, papers, and resins | 75–100 |

Source: Elena Alvárez González, "Algunos efectos en la economía Cubana de los cambios en la conyuntura internacional," Havana: Instituto de Investigaciones Económicas, *mimeo*, June 1991.

food or combustible oils and minerals. Petroleum alone accounted for a third of imports. How far can the government cut before it hits bone?

## The Two-Pronged Strategy for Survival

Cuban policymakers realize that Soviet subsidies are a thing of the past. Policymakers hope to adjust to new realities by reducing import dependence and expanding exports and tourism.

On the import-substitution front, Cuba faces the need for new investment in imported equipment that must be paid for with scarce hard currency. Cutting imports will reduce standards of living even more. Gasoline and diesel fuel are already used mainly by commuter buses or trucks. Bicycles are great for the environment, but it is unrealistic to ask older workers to commute by bike from housing projects several miles outside of Havana. If Castro's plans to import more bicycles from China go through, there will be one bike for every thirteen Cubans by the end of this year. But transportation of food and manufactured goods across Cuba's 600-mile island will require more than strong muscles. Wood, charcoal, and sugar cane waste are being explored as alternative fuels for power generators and vehicles, but not even Cubans can make a 1958 Cadillac run on charcoal. Alcohol, a byproduct of sugar, is used to fuel many Brazilian cars. Brazil's massive investment in alcohol production and subsidies to owners of cars that run on alcohol proved that alcohol is an expensive form of energy compared to oil.

Finding substitutes for imported fabrics, soap, paper, and petroleum will not be easy. Expanding rice production means more irrigation: where will the new equipment come from? Even if land is shifted out of sugar production to produce food, there will be still less hard currency to import essentials.

Oxen have displaced tractors in agriculture, but harvest yields have also fallen.

Cubans believe that dependence on imported fabric might be overcome by growing and weaving cotton. But where will the spinners and looms come from? Transportation could shift from gasoline and diesel to electricity generated by new nuclear power plants. But how will the country buy electric vehicles? Foreign firms know that joint ventures to serve the domestic market will not generate hard currency to remit profits abroad, and they realize that counting on the government to convert peso profits to dollars is a big gamble.

It is true that Cuba has significant unrealized export potential. Expansion however, requires investment. To depress consumption further for the sake of financing new investment in export industries will almost certainly lead to revolt.

Joint ventures are bringing in cash, but so far they have not amounted to much except in tourism. Lack of competitive internal markets puts a damper on foreign firms' interest in joint ventures, because profits are subject to government pricing of inputs, including labor. Attempts to attract capital to export industries are stymied by U.S. threats to exclude participating firms from the U.S. market. Two deals, one with a Spanish tobacco company and another with a Brazilian airline, are said to have fallen through as a result of U.S. pressure.

In the end, Cuba must acknowledge that it is a small, open economy. Its dependence on trade means that it must integrate into the world economy. Doing so requires shifting gears. Trade relations with nonsocialist countries are barely developed. Latin America and Canada, which have well-established diplomatic ties with Cuba, take up only 6 percent of its exports. Moreover, Cuba ran a significant trade deficit that reached 17 percent of national income in 1989. Socialist trade partners picked up most of the tab. They no longer do so. Thus, not only must Cuba find new markets for what it could once sell, but it must also pay for what it buys.

## How Much Can Cuba Sell Abroad?

It is becoming increasingly apparent that former Soviet republics will bow to internal economic pressure and eliminate subsidies to Cuba. Yet Cubans argue that the republics will continue to need Cuban sugar: even if diplomatic relations deteriorate, the republics cannot abandon Cuba as a trade partner.[1] The contrary seems more likely, given the state of the republic economies. In the fall of 1991, Soviet inflation had soared to 1,000 percent, the wheat harvest promised to be smaller than usual, exports of oil had fallen off, and few Soviet enterprises were able to maintain production. The Soviet republics are not in a position to enjoy confections in the next few years. There is simply not enough output to trade for Cuban sugar, given the pressing need to import grains and other essential imports. It will take several years for the republics to get on their feet, and by then most will not need Cuban sugar.

Who will buy Cuban sugar? Can other countries pick up the exports that the USSR and Eastern Europe once absorbed, even at markedly less favorable terms of trade? Cuba can unload all of its sugar in the world market if it is willing to let prices plummet. Table 5.4 shows Cuba's principal trade partners. Europe is self-sufficient in sugar, the United States grants access to its market only as a form of aid, and Japan imports only small quantities. China and Mexico both import Cuban sugar, but are normally net exporters. Potential markets for Cuban sugar include Algeria, Egypt, Iran, Iraq, Israel, Saudi Arabia, Sri Lanka, Syria, and Yemen. Further east,

**Table 5.4**
Cuba's trade partners, 1989

| Importing country or region | Percent of total Cuban exports |
| --- | --- |
| USSR | 60 |
| Other Eastern European countries | 16 |
| EEC | 8 |
| China | 4 |
| Japan | 2 |
| Canada | 2 |
| Other Latin American countries | 4 |
| Rest of the world | 4 |

Source: *Anuario Estadístico de Cuba*, 1989.

Hong Kong, India, and Indonesia are big markets, but the latter two have erratic imports that depend on local harvests. It is little wonder that Cuba initially sided with Iraq in the Persian Gulf War.

Compared to sugar, other Cuban exports bring in a small amount of foreign resources (table 5.5). The main exports are minerals, citrus, tobacco, and fish products. Nickel has proved lucrative in recent years, thanks to high world prices. But, nickel, like sugar, has been sold principally to the USSR. To make matters worse, the U.S. embargo includes steel articles made with Cuban nickel and U.S. steel companies, eager to knock out foreign competitors, have made sure that this provision sticks.

Consider the other products. Citrus output is not easily increased in the short run because trees take several years to mature. Tobacco markets are aggressively held by major international companies. Cuba is losing access to fishing areas. Moreover, even if the export volume of any of these products were to triple, it would not go far toward paying the overall import bill.

**Table 5.5**
Composition of Cuban exports, 1989

|                              | Exports (percent of total exports) |
|------------------------------|:----------------------------------:|
| Reexports of petroleum from USSR | 4.0                            |
| Sugar                        | 72.6                               |
| Nonsugar total               | 23.5                               |
| Metallic minerals and crude iron | 10.5                           |
| Tobacco                      | 1.6                                |
| Citrus fruit                 | 2.6                                |
| Fish products                | 2.4                                |
| Other                        | 6.4                                |

Source: CEPAL, *Estudio económico de América Latina y el Caribe 1989: Cuba*, Santiago, 1990.

What can be said about high tech exports? Cuba has exported computer components to Eastern Europe. That market has all but dried up, and there is not a whisper of hope that this sector can now make a difference. Biotechnology has proved more lucrative, but this is a rapidly changing field. Cuba's ability to remain competitive depends on whether multinational firms choose to undercut its market, and whether it can maintain cooperative relations with scientists in developed countries. Cuba's violations of international patents in biotechnology reduce its access to European and Japanese markets. Developing countries offer a limited market for high-priced drugs like interferon: although Cuba undercuts international prices by more than 50 percent, a course of interferon treatment for hepatitis B costs $1,404 per patient. Its highly touted vaccine for meningitis was marketed without proper clinical trials and turned out to be ineffective against the strains prevalent in Brazil. The Pan-American

Health Organization has indicated concern about the safety of new Cuban drugs.

Cuban policymakers hope to triple tourism revenues by 1995, from $250 million in 1990. Yet Cuban economists note that for every dollar a tourist spends, Cuba must spend 38 cents to import the luxuries—televisions, swimming pool filters, scotch, and soap—that keep the tourist happy. There is not enough electricity now. Will hotel lights burn while the rest of Havana fumbles in the dark?

**Retrenchment**

Rationing now covers virtually all consumer goods. As of June 1991, the daily bread ration was just 3 ounces per person. Eggs were limited to nine per fortnight, and meat was simply out of the question. Layoffs were being used to avoid excess liquidity in the system and to pressure workers to agree to work in the countryside.

Last year Castro claimed that Cuba would face this crisis, "without putting anyone onto the streets, without depriving a single citizen of his resources, and without leaving anyone unemployed. . . . If we must reduce the work week, we will reduce it. If we cannot work five days, we will work four. And if we cannot work four, we will work three and give time off."[2] Do Cubans want jobs, or do they want to earn a living? If there are no goods to buy, few will show up even for a three-day workweek.

How long will it take before people ask, what is the point of stubbornly running the economy into the ground? Equality? That is already going by the boards with new ventures that offer special incentives. Insurance against starvation? Even poor Chileans who lived off meager make-work stipends during the Pinochet years could afford 3 ounces of bread a day. Nationalist pride is eroding as joint ventures with foreign firms dominate the most successful sectors of the economy. Soon Cubans will ask why foreigners are invited to make investments that Cubans are prohibited from making. As the state clamps down on Cubans' scramble for survival, it will not take long before they resist restrictions.

Looking the other way as black markets emerge is one way to fill the gaps. Then what will Cuba have gained? Speculation and hoarding will deprive many Cubans of basic goods, while others profit wildly. The formal economy will bow to the illegal economy, with no job security and no regulation to protect people. The risk of arrest in the black market will thwart investment, stifle the growth of real output, and encourage corruption. If there is one model that is worth avoiding, it is the chaotic hoarding, strikes, and shortages that marred the last days of Allende's socialist regime in Chile.

**The Road to Capitalism**

Is it possible to build capitalism while maintaining social progress? Cuba must now take the lead in demonstrating how capitalism can be tamed. The task confronting Cuba is to build capitalism from the wreckage of its socialist system, while securing political support for policies that will make most Cubans worse off in the short run. It will not be easy. Despite the benefits of unification, East Germany's transition to capitalism was tougher than expected: output plunged, unemployment increased, and enterprises that were once showcase earners of hard currency were disbanded. Just as it was difficult to impose communism upon capitalist Cuba so will it be hard to install a functioning capitalist system after three decades of communism. As Cuba discards central planning, removes price controls, ends subsidies, and sells public enterprises, the pain and tumult will be excruciating. Trading Castro for aid might smooth the transition, but unemployment, deteriorating welfare programs, and falling real wages may create revolt.

In every transition from socialism to capitalism, economists' recipe for success includes a set of common steps. Government must create a stable fiscal environment, liberalize trade and prices, and privatize. These broad guidelines go along with reform of the monetary system, the establishment of new taxation schemes, new laws on foreign investment, as well as protection of intellectual property and safeguards for consumers. It is hoped that the new environment will bring in foreign capital and the helping hand of loans at favorable interest rates. Two factors determine the outcome of reforms: the political legitimacy of the transition, and economic policies. As economists, it is easier for us to talk about the latter, although nearly every economic policy is doomed if it lacks political support.

Will popular support be lacking for capitalism, viewed by many Cubans as the antithesis of social justice? Cubans can study the options. Socialism not only falls short in offering fantasies of extravagant wealth—the opiate of the poor in market economies—it does not even deliver humble luxuries such as lipstick. Until the crisis, socialism was attractive because it fed everyone, guaranteed basic education and health care, and minimized job insecurity. Once things go wrong, the system cannot maintain the education and health care it proudly put forth before, nor supply balanced meals. Strong social mores in Cuba still keep kids from selling themselves on the street as prostitutes as they do in Brazil, but this black market might also emerge as shortages take a harsher toll.

Capitalism can bring many ills, including the extreme inequality that lies at the root of poverty in Brazil and Peru. In

Brazil, the top 10 percent of the population siphons off 46 percent of household income. Among the Latin American countries with the most poverty and repression are Haiti, Guatemala, and Honduras. In these countries, more than half of the population cannot afford a basic food basket. But it is also clear that extreme poverty and repression do not promote growth, not even in profits. Firms are not clamoring to invest in these countries, despite low wages. Capitalism is only partly responsible for the mess; equally to blame are racism, social values, and shortsightedness of political leaders, which prevent these societies from redistributing income. None have decent tax systems, and social spending is wasted on programs that fail to reach the poor.

In the late 1970s, the shortcomings of central planning in socialist economies led Cuba and East European countries to experiment with markets and prices as a coordinating mechanism. Raising the price of individual goods was to signal higher demand and stimulate output of a good. "Market socialism" was believed to be compatible with state ownership and control of production. When market socialism failed as entrepreneurs competed with the state for resources, Cuba reverted to centralization in 1986. In Eastern Europe, attempts at market socialism made clear that decentralization does not solve the problem of incentives in socialism. Homogeneous wage structures tend to stifle efficiency. To transform bureaucrats into entrepreneurs, firms must face the risk of business failure, and the market must be allowed to reward success. Enterprises have to be privatized.

There is no middle way between communism and capitalism, and there is no capitalism without capitalists. The idea that market economies can be created by merely freeing prices has been discredited. Even if free prices can be used to signal the direction for resource allocation, these signals tend to be ignored unless resources are privately owned. Thus without privatization, markets cannot operate.

Efficient allocation of domestic resources is only part of the challenge. A small, open, and poor country like Cuba needs to attract foreign capital to build its productive capacity, and it must become internationally competitive if it is to earn vital foreign exchange. Prices and profits drive global markets: if Cuba wants to play ball in an increasingly capitalist world, it must develop a system that responds quickly to change.

**Privatization**

Throughout Latin America, with the exception of Cuba, public ownership of key sectors has come under sharp scrutiny. Reaganomics, Thatcherism, the debt crisis, and the collapse of the socialist economies of Eastern Europe have spurred a fresh interest in free-market economics. Privatization fever has risen with the perceived failure of state intervention and import substitution, as well as with economic stagnation and insurmountable budget deficits. State-owned enterprises are seen as a major source of political patronage and corruption, no longer the beachheads of social progress.

Today, a decade of experience provides some early lessons on the effectiveness of privatization. So far, Latin America's experience suggests that privatization, although no panacea, can be an essential ingredient in mobilizing resources for growth.

Not all Latin American countries have combined their rhetoric about privatization with action. Most countries have paid lip service to privatization; few have actually reformed the public sector. As part of their economic reform packages, both Chile and Mexico have been most successful in privatizing large segments of their public sectors. Argentina has also experienced important successes despite fierce labor opposition and a relatively poor economic situation.

In Bolivia and Brazil, rhetoric has far outstripped action. Bolivia's efforts have been stymied by the usual coalition of bureaucratic and political forces that view privatization with alarm. In essence, privatization in Bolivia has amounted to little more than a reorganization of the state control over the economy. Brazil's large state-run sector has likewise been slow to shrink. The governments of Jose Sarney and Fernando Collor offered a menu of privatization schemes in a bid to rein in the fiscal deficit and inflation. But the net result has been modest. Collor's promise to "privatize one enterprise a month" has not reduced the size of the state.

Compared to the effort required in Cuba, privatization elsewhere in Latin America seems an easy task. The public sector in Cuba represents the bulk of output. Cobblers, bars, vending stands, and auto repair shops were taken over in 1968, in an effort to wipe out what Castro saw as the parasitic nature of the petite bourgeoisie. In contrast, even in Mexico where public ownership was widespread until the mid-1980s, it amounted to only 17 percent of GDP. In Latin America, companies can be privatized one by one, while in Cuba most public enterprises will have to be privatized simultaneously to create a functioning market economy.

Rapid privatization means fire-sale prices. Chile took this route in the 1970s. Suspicion still remains that the shares were sold at less than their true worth and that Pinochet's cronies were able to cut special deals. Financial liberalization took an extreme form and ignored prudent regulation. Credit demand was biased toward high-risk firms, and banks employed risky lending strategies. The result was high unemployment and a spate of bankruptcies. The Chilean process was improved after 1983 through efforts to diffuse ownership and screen prospective buyers.

Mexico chose a gradualist approach. Between 1983 and 1985, the government shut down nonviable enterprises. It then privatized small and medium-sized firms, but it only undertook to privatize the large projects in 1988. Gaining experience by privatizing smaller firms first reduces errors when privatizing larger companies.

Gradualism, too slow for the zealots, assures a better prospect of sustainable privatization in most of Latin America. But does the lesson fit Cuba? Programs in the rest of Latin America have been carried out in established market economies. Slow privatization in Cuba will mean that early purchases are made in the presence of strong state control over the economy, and thus offer prices will be low. Moreover, unless foreign trade is immediately liberalized, the privatized enterprises will lack a competitive environment. Gradualism will carry a high cost in Cuba.

How can quick privatization be achieved? The conundrum is that to create a market economy there must be private ownership, but to create private ownership there must be a market. Setting prices is a problem because the value of firms whose shares are not actively traded must be imputed. If their assets cannot be valued, shares can be given away to citizens, who supposedly already own these firms. Poland and Czechoslovakia have begun to privatize by distributing assets freely, or for a nominal charge, across wide segments of the population.

If shares are distributed broadly, however, insiders may abuse their knowledge and undermine the purpose of the distribution. Monitoring of share trading and public disclosure of company performance is necessary to build confidence among stockholders. One widely discussed possibility is to assign ownership of the enterprises (divided, where necessary, into competitively-sized units) to a series of mutual funds, and give an equal number of shares in these funds to each adult.[3] As everyone would start with the same package of mutual fund shares, the system would be fair, and perceived as such. Moreover, people could more easily evaluate a small number of mutual funds, as opposed to shares dispersed in thousands of individual enterprises. The active trading of mutual funds would put pressure on mutual fund managers to secure value from the enterprises in which they invest.

The main barrier to distributing title is that, by the time privatization occurs, the state will be so deeply in the red that it will need the revenues from privatization to maintain essential operations. Thus Cuban citizens are likely to start off with few assets in a transition to capitalism.

Small enterprises can be sold to existing operators. But lack of local savings means that most big enterprises will be sold to foreigners, who have the capital to invest in modernization. Hostility to foreign investment has faded over the past decade, and most Latin American countries are currently modifying their investment regulations in a bid to attract foreign capital. Cuba will have to follow the same route.

Cuba could easily sell its sugar plantations. This would bring a windfall of revenue if the United States could be convinced to extend concessional quotas to Cuba. The government can also cut big deals in unloading electric utilities, telephone, mining, banking, and airline industries. Foreign firms may pick up a few meatpacking, cement, toiletry, and textile plants, but much of the existing manufacturing base is small and equipment is outdated. Investment in this area is more likely to take the form of new investment—perhaps with some purchases of existing buildings and warehouses—rather than genuine privatization of existing operations.

A few industries are critical to the success of the rest of the economy. Cuba cannot risk selling utilities, banks, or transportation systems to poor managers, particularly because some of this infrastructure is already in bad shape. The price of these assets cannot be the sole factor determining the government's choice among bidders. The government has to ensure that privatization is made to consortia with the capacity to attract capital, management, and technology. The conflict between auctioning to the highest bidder and the need to ensure that firms are acquired by sound investors can be solved in a two-step procedure: unacceptable bidders are sorted out according to qualitative criteria before the public auction is held. Mexico routinely evaluates bidders, and the possibility of barring certain candidates from a given sale is already established in Brazil.

To ensure that bidding conditions are appropriate, that the valuation of the assets is realistic, and that reliable information on financial markets is given due consideration when establishing the financial conditions, privatization requires both recognized international industry specialists and financial advisers. As an example, the most controversial issue surrounding Chilean privatization was the value of the sales themselves. Shares were sold at their market values quoted in the stock exchange, as opposed to their book values. Book values were deemed irrelevant, whereas market values reflected risk and expected profits in an economy that was deeply depressed. If Cuba privatizes gradually, uncertainty about the availability of inputs and the macroeconomic environment will make it difficult even for independent assessors to gauge value. Charges of corruption must be kept to a minimum by opening the process to public scrutiny.

Once the government has decided to offer a plant for sale, there is little logic in trying to improve the price by devoting time and expertise to a restructuring task better accomplished by a new buyer. Most prospective buyers can imagine what the plant would look like once painted; few would be fooled by a fresh coat of paint. Of course, measures such as eliminating subsidies and solving legal problems (labor contracts, for instance) must be taken before a firm is ready for privatization.

## The Regulatory Environment

Legal rules are a common good allowing coordination of individual actions. Erratic, discretionary rules and privileged access to public officials limit the ability of firms to make contracts, and thus produce economic losses. Impartial mechanisms for law enforcement, such as courts and arbitration systems, are essential to facilitate private contracting. Neutrally enforced legislation presumes a stable government committed to the existing legal framework.

The establishment of private property requires defining the legal forms of nonstate organizations, such as individual proprietorship, limited liability joint stock companies, and legal stipulations on the rights and limitations of private ownership. But the need for a new legal framework does not stop there. Unfettered markets can bring rampant pollution, unsafe conditions for workers, hazards to consumers, and the abuse of market power.

Land-use planning is essential to avoid the tendency toward overdevelopment in tourist areas. Green spaces must be preserved between hotels if tourists are not to feel like rats in multistory cages. Left to their own devices, hotel proprietors will design sewerage systems that pollute the very waters they advertise. Each hotel's effluent is only a small part of the problem, but the total effect can destroy a beach. Air pollution in Havana, runoff from pesticides in agriculture, and toxic solid waste all call for state intervention to protect a common good.

Workers need information about the risks they take, and protection from gross exploitation, especially where high unemployment breeds desperation. Consumers and competing firms must have recourse to deal with sausages filled with sawdust. Will capitalist Cuba recreate the world of Upton Sinclair? Caveat emptor is the rule in most capitalist developing countries, for governments lack the resources to enforce all laws. The best one can hope for is a state that targets the most egregious violations.

As much as the state needs to step out of its role in production to stimulate growth, it must take on the responsibility of establishing a clear regulatory structure, particularly for newly established private monopolies. Utilities do not function in contestable markets: electricity, telephone, and water services need price regulation to make up for the absence of competitive pressure.

A sound legal structure is not antithetical to foreign investment. It ensures businesses that their long-term investments will not be ruined by arbitrary political decisions. But there is a fine line between establishing the rules of fair play and bureaucratic meddling. If businesses doubt a country's stability or fear regulatory reversals, they will refuse to play the game, and privatization efforts will be sharply restricted.

**Economic Reform**

Privatization is merely one act in a larger play. The reversal of decades of statism in Chile by the regime of General Pinochet has created the basis of what is arguably the healthiest economy in the region. Although not as far-reaching, Mexico's privatization scheme stands as a more rational method to reduce the size of the state. Central to the success of both economies has been trade liberalization and fiscal stabilization.

Trade liberalization is essential to create competitive pressure in the domestic market and to prevent balance-of-payments crises. Cubans will not fare much better than they do now if imports are restricted to prop up local firms. Under the highly protectionist policies that prevailed between 1940 and 1980, Latin Americans paid several times the world price of goods that fell under import quotas. Cuba is a relatively small economy. Consequently, to achieve economies of scale, most industries must ultimately export. Creating protectionist barriers will simply slow progress toward competitiveness. Barriers to entry and difficult access to intermediate inputs from abroad will also stifle foreign investment.

Table 5.6 shows the growing budget deficits of the Cuban government. Fiscal imbalances drive most of the economic instability in Latin America. Unable or unwilling to tax, governments print money to pay their bills. Excessive monetary growth produces inflation. Inflation is repressed by price controls, but when they are eliminated, inflation erupts. Tax reform is key to mopping up the red ink on fiscal ledgers. Most countries are turning to a value-added tax, which is somewhat self-enforcing, because firms benefit by reporting purchases from other firms. It is also less distorting than

**Table 5.6**
Government revenues and expenditures as share of Cuban GSP, 1986–1989 (percent)

|                        | 1986 | 1987 | 1988 | 1989 |
|------------------------|------|------|------|------|
| Total expenditures     | 44.3 | 46.8 | 48.1 | 51.9 |
| Current expenditures   | 32.7 | 36.6 | 38.0 | 40.4 |
| Investment             | 11.6 | 10.2 | 10.1 | 11.5 |
| Revenues               | 43.6 | 44.4 | 43.7 | 46.7 |
| Deficit                | 0.7  | 2.4  | 4.4  | 5.2  |

Source: CEPAL, *Estudio económico de América Latina y el Caribe 1989: Cuba*, Santiago, 1990.

customs taxes. Although it is less progressive than a graduated income tax, Latin American countries (and most European countries) have found that compliance is better. If Cuba moves quickly, it has a shot at establishing a workable taxation scheme to finance basic social spending.

## Monetary Overhang

Under socialism, planners decide about production and distribution, but workers receive their income in money while consumers both pay for goods with money and store savings in money. In a market economy, when the government prints too much money, prices increase. In a socialist economy, when enterprise losses are covered by the fiscal budget and money creation, households will hold the excess money balances (involuntary savings). With shortages, the money cannot be used to buy goods at controlled prices, unless a parallel economy is allowed to emerge. In this case, money leaks into the parallel market, pushing up prices. Cuba created a parallel market in 1973, when the state began to sell surplus goods at prices above those of rationed goods. But in general the parallel market is not enough to eliminate the "monetary overhang" in socialist economies. When the transition to a market economy begins, it releases a burst of inflation. Social tension develops as real incomes change because prices and wages rise at different rates. Inflation diverts energy from real production to financial scams. In the end, there is less output. If the government is using inflationary finance in a feeble effort to redistribute income, the poor will not gain much. They have no accounts in Miami that are safe from rising prices.

Inflation also wreaks havoc on the balance of payments. The exchange rate inevitably becomes overvalued, for no government uses a completely free-floating currency. Exports suffer and imports become artificially cheap. Some banks may be foolish enough to cover the trade deficit with loans, but investors will shy away from chaotic exchange rates.

In Cuba, the monetary system has created a currency from which people will flee as soon as they can. Pesos have been printed in excess, and thus the monetary economy is out of pace with the real economy. A black market for dollars[4] emerged with the revolution in early 1959, and the volume of average daily transactions reached more than 100,000 pesos in the spring of 1960. In 1961 all circulating money was replaced, and no individual was allowed to exchange more than 200 pesos, thus achieving a major reduction in the money supply. Despite these measures and heavy penalties, black market activity continued. The dollar exchange rate jumped to a record high of 25 pesos in 1963. After 1967, black market dealings shrank and the premium fell sharply. At the end of 1969, only the smallest quantities of Cuban pesos would find buyers abroad, and Miami had ceased dealing in them.

In the 1980s, with more tourists from hard-currency countries visiting Cuba, and with Cubans holding more pesos that could buy nothing at official prices, the volume of dealings in the black market increased again. Economic deterioration in the late 1980s brought with it a renewed fall in the value of the peso (figure 5.1). The country now lacks a credible currency for a transition to a market economy.

Monetary reform is one mechanism for reducing outstanding cash balances. In Latin America, most monetary reforms misfired because populist governments, unable to combine the monetary reform with austerity, relied on price controls to stop inflation. The inti in Peru, the austral in Argentina, the cruzado in Brazil, and the cordoba oro in Nicaragua were all failed attempts to reestablish confidence in the local currency.

Source: Pick's Currency Yearbook

**Figure 5.1**

Each flopped because governments continued to finance large deficits with money creation. In its first attempts at perestroika, the Soviet Union also made the mistake of trying to dampen consumer outrage by subsidizing prices. The fiscal deficit rose from 2.5 percent of GDP in 1985 to 11 percent in 1988. Monetary growth, which doubled over the course of the decade, financed the deficit.[5] The consequence was monetary overhang and repressed inflation.

Cuba also suffers from monetary overhang. A fund for monetary reform, financed through the International Monetary Fund, would help to stabilize the peso by making it convertible into Western currencies. A convertible peso is essential for foreign investors to transform profits into currencies they can use. Private investment is the best hope for Cuba's economic salvation, and it will only come as the economy reforms with the help of foreign governments.

Monetary and budgetary restraint is necessary to prevent inflation from undermining structural adjustment loans. This means that the Cuban government will have a hard time financing social programs during a shift to capitalism.

## Social Welfare

Cuban workers raised on large doses of socialist ideology will not buy a wholehearted shift to a market economy—they want their free education, daycare, and health benefits. Will growth in the first years be thwarted by instant class conflict? How effective will the political leadership be in unifying popular support for a transition to capitalism?

Stable economic growth requires fiscal restraint. Cuba will not be able to afford to maintain unviable enterprises, to offer all families free health care, and to subsidize basic foods. Even if socialism persists, the state will be limited in how much it can deliver.

Hard choices will have to be made. A progressive government will cut subsidies to university education before it cuts primary school teachers. It will let the price of gasoline rise before it closes clinics that provide basic immunizations. And it will ensure that electricity rates reflect the cost of generation.

Given a very tight budget, redistributive programs must target the poor. Subsidized universities and gasoline mainly benefit the middle class, which will have to start paying its own way. Even subsidies of basic foods involve too much leakage. For every very poor Cuban who benefits from subsidized milk, five others who could afford to pay the full cost of production pay practically nothing.

Direct transfer payments, such as welfare checks in the United States, are administratively cumbersome because ascertaining incomes is difficult. But first priorities are clear: sanitation programs, potable water, decent primary schools, and clinics that can treat diarrhea, dispense birth control pills, and immunize children are at the top of the list. Cuba now does well in these areas. The challenge is to maintain these accomplishments.

Privatization has an important impact on the distribution of wealth, which will drive social welfare for decades. Privatization carries social costs that derive from potential variations in employment patterns implicit in ownership change. Labor has resisted privatization with good reason: the logical first step in cutting losses is to cut the payroll. The sale of a given percentage of shares to workers on favorable credit terms overcomes workers' opposition and helps to bring about productivity increases. A small number of worker ownership schemes have been set up in Chile and Costa Rica. The main challenge is financing such programs, because few workers can raise sufficient capital.

Filling state coffers with the proceeds from privatization can ease fiscal problems, but it can also finance fiscal mismanagement and corruption. When President Carlos Salinas annnounced the privatization of Mexican banks, he argued that the money from assets sales was necessary to attack poverty. The opposition was by and large rendered speechless. Salinas keeps his hand out of the till, but the PRI (Institutional Revolutionary Party[6]) does not resist the temptation to buy votes by using public spending to its political advantage.

The poorest have the least political power, and thus politicians easily lose sight of them as budgets are set. Riots at the University of Havana, strikes, and populist political maneuvering would make backsliding inevitable. Will Cuba look like Costa Rica, where democracy and greater equality have taken root? Or will it look like Guatemala, where poverty rates are high, income is inequitably distributed, and repression is routine?

## Who Will Foot the Bill?

Some people believe that if Cuba relents and shifts toward capitalism, the United States will step in with massive aid. This is unlikely. As long as Castro is in power, there will be no U.S. aid. He is deeply distrusted by the Washington establishment. Aid might also send a signal to the rest of Latin America that there is no penalty for three decades of harangues against the United States, thus setting off a new round of populist demagoguery in the region.

Even if Castro leaves power, there will be no flood of aid. Budget problems in the United States, growing opposition to foreign aid,[7] and bigger crises elsewhere in the world put Cuba in a weak negotiating position. Instability in the Soviet republics poses a potentially far graver threat, the solution to which will require aid on the scale of the Marshall Plan. As a former pawn in the rivalry between the two superpowers, Cuba has no clout.

What about a remake of the Puerto Rican experience? Might Cuba slip into a cozy relationship with the United States? Neither Cubans nor Americans relish the idea of a return to a quasi-colonial relationship. Puerto Rico is seen as an economic burden. Most Puerto Ricans either work for the government or depend on U.S. social security. The United States spends $3 billion a year in direct transfers to the island. Statehood is now almost certain to be rejected by the United States, for Republicans are not eager to pay welfare checks to liberal Puerto Ricans. Indeed, Congress is already talking about weaning Puerto Rico from dependence by withdrawing Section 936 privileges, which grant tax breaks to manufacturers on the island.

What would the United States get for its money in Cuba? In rejecting socialism, East Germany was embraced by its neighbor. But West Germans yearned for reunification of their culture, their families, and their patrimony. Unlike the relationship between East and West Germany, Cuba is not part of the American soul.

Nicaraguans had hoped for help from the United States as a reward for electing Violeta Chamorro to the presidency in April 1990. But a year later, the United States was still dragging its feet on aid. When violence broke out in 1991, with Sandinistas calling the shots, the United States finally acted to prevent a collapse of stability in the region. In April 1991, Congress approved a $300 million aid package.

Panama fared no better, although its control over the canal gives it more strategic significance. Although the United States promised $500 million after the invasion of December 1989, Panama had received only $32 million a year later. Charges that Panama continues to serve as a drug haven have stalled further aid. Constant popular protests refer to Endara as a traitor for his failure to deliver enough help from the United States.

In short, the United States alone will not carry the ball. Under the best circumstances, Cuba might get as much as $1 billion from the United States within the first few years of a transition to capitalism. However, other sources of financing include the World Bank, the Inter-American Development Bank, and the International Monetary Fund, as well as countries that have avoided Cuba for political reasons. Taiwan is now a significant donor to Nicaragua, for it hopes to begin manufacturing there. The big money, if there is going to be any, will be private money.

**Foreign Capital**

For the time being, additional commercial loans are unlikely given Cuba's overextended financial situation. Cuba has borrowed up to its neck. It owes $18 billion (in rubles) to the Soviet Union and countries in the East bloc, and $6 billion to Western commercial banks.[8] Debt to the East bloc may be put on softer terms, but commercial banks are not budging. Now that the threat of widespread financial collapse has ebbed, commercial banks are holding out for stiff rescheduling conditions before they agree to new loans. On the whole, banks are lending very little to Latin American countries. They will not be the first to step in with money for a capitalist startup.

The government is presently pursuing joint ventures with foreign firms, mostly in tourism. The justification is that these firms are teaching Cubans how to get tourism off the ground. Throughout the 1950s and 1960s, Latin American governments set up joint ventures in pharmaceuticals, automobiles, mining, and a host of other industries. Typically the government retained 51 percent ownership. To be willing to relinquish control of the plant, foreign firms either required guaranteed profits, or they let the government put up most of the capital while they served as managers. Cuba can attract firms, but can it get them to put money up front? Or is the government mainly buying foreign expertise? It has very little cash left to afford joint ventures that do not bring in new cash. Nor does it have a deep pocket to absorb the risks of failed enterprises. A clean sale of assets will make more sense as the country shifts toward open markets.

Cuban exiles are a potential source of cash: Nicaragua's "Miami boys" are already helping to revive that economy. For the most part, Cuban-American entrepreneurs run small operations. They won't come in if they are doubtful about the economic climate because they do not have enough negotiating power to deal with adverse policy changes. To attract these firms, Cuba needs to establish a credible and stable political environment, and to reduce bureaucratic red tape to a minimum.

Cuba now faces grim choices. Without Soviet aid, Cuban socialism cannot provide people with a decent standard of living. A shift to capitalism offers Cuba the chance to expand its trade relations with other market economies, including its biggest potential trade partner, the United States. Foreign investors wait in the wings. How much money they bring in depends on whether the government can provide secure property rights, reliable infrastructure, stable exchange rates, and cooperative trade relations with other countries. The extent to which capitalist growth benefits poor Cubans depends on how the government sets up the transition: it must not miss the opportunity to create a sound tax structure and carefully targeted social programs. Passivity will not pay. Only dramatic changes in the Cuban economy will realize people's dreams of a better life.

# 6    In the U.S. Interest

As the Soviet Union changes from an adversary to an ally of the United States, the threat of communism disappears. The implications go well beyond Soviet-American relations. Is it possible to resolve the United States' differences with Cuba?

In Washington, power brokers argue that to open negotiations while Castro is in power is to offer the tyrant a cure that would raise him from his deathbed. Some say that Cuba not only rejects U.S. demands to free political prisoners and hold elections, but it also refuses dialogue and negotiates in bad faith. As a matter of fact, Cubans have proved they can keep commitments. Since 1984, a migration agreement has led to the repatriation of Cuban criminals and exit visas for former political prisoners. Cuba agreed to withdraw all troops from Angola in 1988, and in May 1991 the last Cuban soldier left that country. Cuban support for guerrillas in Central America is now minimal. The best way to move Cuba toward desirable policies is to remain engaged and to influence the changes that will inevitably take place.

## The Military Issue

The thirty-year-old policy toward Cuba is musty. In 1991, the notion that an island of 10.5 million people threatens a superpower of 250 million is silly. Should the United States invade Cuba? The Gulf War gave the United States confidence in its military abilities and demonstrated the decline of Soviet hegemony. Despite the high cost of a U.S. invasion, some are bold enough to believe that an invasion will happen, an idea that was shelved after the Bay of Pigs debacle. One senses that Cuban diplomats are wary of providing the right pretext: if Cuba appears too strong, it is a potential threat to hemispheric stability. If it seems on the verge of collapse, U.S. soldiers can expect to be met with cheering in the streets. Even if the United States stays out of Cuba, changes in the strategic balance between the United States and the Soviet Union force Cuba to spend more money on its own defense, thus fueling its economic crisis.

Although the Gulf War proved an immense boon to George Bush's popularity, an invasion of Cuba would be a gross mistake in terms of the the U.S. interests in the region, and it might well fail to swiftly depose Castro, as the Gulf War failed to depose Saddam Hussein. U.S. military intervention is unnecessary because the current system is already showing signs of weakness. Invasion would carry a very high price for the United States' image in Latin America, and it would either simply advance a process that is already under way, or provide a catalyst for renewed propaganda against U.S. imperialism and rally support for Castro. The problem of removing foes and dictators is always followed by the thorny dilemma of how to replace them.

Nuclear power complicates the strategic equation. Cuba's arsenal, if it exists at all, is not big enough to attack without devastating retaliation. No sane Cuban leader would strike first. A more serious nuclear threat may lie in the construction of nuclear power plants, expected to come on-line soon. Americans are already edgy about the possibility of a

Chernobyl-type accident. Indeed, this is a likely pretext for an unwise invasion before the U.S. presidential elections in 1992. U.S. officials debate where Cuba's nuclear plan leads. By mid-1991 Cuba was installing twin 440,000-kilowatt Soviet reactors and had in storage a 10,000-kilowatt Soviet research reactor, which uses highly enriched uranium fuel. Some U.S. officials worry about the weapon potential of enriched uranium used in the research reactor. Others minimize the danger posed by the reactor because its output of plutonium, which could be used to build nuclear weapons, is so small that it would take years to produce enough for a bomb. The U.S. Nuclear Regulatory Commission's Harold Denton, who managed the Three Mile Island crisis, said the reactors Cuba is installing are much safer than the reactor that caused the accident at Chernobyl.[1] The twin reactors do not meet U.S. requirements for protection against fire and earthquakes, but they exceed U.S. standards in other safety respects such as the size of their cooling systems.

On September 11, 1991, President Mikhail Gorbachev announced that Moscow was opening talks with Havana to withdraw 11,000 Soviet troops from the island. The Kremlin hoped that the withdrawal would be matched by a removal of U.S. forces at Guantánamo Bay. The United States would face no costs in agreeing to leave Guantánamo Bay, a move long requested by Havana. The Guantánamo Naval Base is the only American installation in communist territory, an artificial piece of America on foreign soil, supplied by barges that arrive twice a month from Florida with toys, frozen waffles, and disposable diapers. It is the oldest U.S. military installation outside the United States. Some 6,000 U.S. military personnel are based there, and marines in battle dress stand twenty-four-hour guard along heavily fortified fences.

Under the terms of an indefinite lease negotiated in 1903 and renewed in 1934, the land reverts to Cuban control only if abandoned or by mutual consent. Cuba contends that the agreements were obtained by coercion and that the base threatens its security and national sovereignty. Cuba does not cash the $4,085 rent checks that the United States sends every year. American military analysts agree that the base has little strategic importance. It is difficult to justify pouring tax dollars into Guantánamo. The military once argued that the expenses of the base ($34 million in 1990) were necessary to keep it out of Soviet hands. Now that the Soviets have lost interest in Cuba, this argument is no longer valid. It is time for the United States to get out and let Club Med move in. With its natural beauty, Guantánamo can play a part in tourism and generate far more for Cuba than a few thousand dollars.

Cubans are fed up with their own system, but their fierce nationalism, so evident in the Pan-American Games, should not be underestimated. The U.S. military presence in Cuba has been a sore point for ninety years; even the initial lease was grudgingly signed. Guantánamo's land belongs to Cuba, and Cubans want the right to evict their tenant. When Castro goes—if not before—so should the base.

## Trade and Tourism

Only ninety miles from Florida, Cuba remains isolated as a result of the U.S. economic boycott. In 1962 the United States persuaded the countries of the Organization of American States (OAS), with the exception of Mexico, to end commerce with Cuba. At the same time, international financial institutions withheld credit.

The embargo represented a major destabilizing shock for the Cuban economy. At the end of the 1950s, Cuba sent 71 percent of its exports to the United States and depended on the United States for 64 percent of its imports. After the revolution, the Soviet Union stepped in. Cuba's economic isolation in the Western Hemisphere began to ease in the mid-1970s when the OAS voted to lift the economic and diplomatic embargo. The Reagan administration tightened the embargo, contending that it denied Cuba hard currency that could be used to support subversive overseas activities. Resuming trade between the two countries would be an important part of restoring relations, but it is unlikely that trade will return to its 1950s proportions: there is a limited U.S. market for Cuban exports, and the Japanese and Europeans now export far more industrial goods than they did thirty years ago. But the proximity of the two countries creates many opportunities for trade, and tourism would certainly revive.

How should U.S. policy toward Cuba change, now that the Cold War is over? How is it likely to change? These are two different questions. Answers to the former are plainly colored by the ideology of two different groups. And answers to the second question depend on which group is able to put together the most convincing arguments and pressure that shape Washington's decisions.

There is clearly a trade-off between maintaining the embargo to force change in Cuba and enduring opposition to such a policy. Thus the debate on the embargo takes two sides. One side argues that the United States should not intervene in other countries' affairs unless strategically threatened. Cuba itself is unlikely to pose a military threat to the United States: its past threat resulted from its potential as a Soviet beachhead. With that threat at an end, this justification for maintaining the embargo is at best very weak. Moreover, many countries whose policies are anathema to the United States maintain open trade relations with the United States. Castro's human rights record is questionable, but it is not nearly as bad as that of dictators whom the United States has financed in El Salvador, Guatemala, and Honduras, to name only a few examples in Latin America. China has recently been granted most-favored-nation status in trade relations with the United States, despite the Tiananmen Square massacre and a continued nuclear buildup.

Proponents of diplomatic restraint argue that there is more influence to be gained by opening economic ties to Cuba than by continuing to isolate the country. In the first place, the U.S. policy prevents change by helping to keep Cuba's nationalist spirit alive. The United States offers itself as the absolute enemy that can be used to justify all types of control and be blamed for anything that goes wrong on the island. The image of Yankee hostility upholds Castro's rule. Current policy gives Castro the benefit of painting the United States as the global oppressor. U.S. interests would be advanced by putting him to the test of no excuses.

By prohibiting travel to Cuba, the United States helps rather than hurts repression there. More contact between Cuban and American citizens would foster democratic change: Americans traveling to Cuba could talk, bring in videocassettes and fax machines—in short, the same communications technology that helped to destroy the wall of isolation around Eastern Europe.

Trade relations would make it possible to engage in creative diplomacy and dialogue. Access to the U.S. market is a powerful lure: look at the changes Salinas is making in electoral process and environmental policy to expand U.S.-Mexico trade relations. Current policy hamstrings the United States in its ability to shape the destiny of Cuba after communism. Closer economic ties can help to establish the relationships that will be necessary to jump-start the economy once communism falls.

It is true, as Castro's opponents argue, that the embargo puts pressure on a dictator that has proven his willingness to act as a strategic host to the most powerful enemy of United States. Elections are held, but Castro does not put h own power at stake. His rhetoric has long advocated an over-throw of capitalism. Nonetheless complete isolation aids Castro's efforts to make fanatic socialist monks of the Cubans.

As much as an invasion would be a mistake, so too would a policy of ignoring Cuba. As the largest country in the Caribbean, Cuba offers potentially important leadership in a region beset by poverty and instability. It is a promising source of economic growth in the region. Moreover, violence and economic collapse in Cuba could easily start a massive exodus in the direction of Miami. Stability in Cuba is in the best interest of the United States.

Presently, U.S. policymakers are unlikely to unilaterally lift the economic embargo against Cuba. Precisely because Cuba is now insignificant in geopolitics, they see no reason to change policy. Lifting the embargo would raise the ire of powerful conservatives while yielding little political benefit for the Bush administration. The United States does not need Cuban sugar or access to Cuban beaches. Nor is there much incentive to coopt the Castro regime to reduce Cuba's role as a symbol of rebellion in the Western hemisphere. Indeed, Cuba now stands as a lesson to other Latin American leaders, especially as the economy collapses.

## Cuban-Americans

With the exception of the massive Mariel boatlift in 1980, Cuban refugees have fit into the United States. According to the *Financial Times* (September 13, 1991), the Soviet decision to withdraw troops from Cuba represents the first fruits of intensive contact between reformers in Moscow and the politically influential Cuban-American community in the

United States. A measure of their influence is seen in the treatment of Cuban immigrants. Mexicans, Jamaicans, Haitians, and other immigrants from Western nations who arrive illegally in the United States are returned home unless they are granted political asylum, which few manage to obtain. Cuban refugees are dealt with differently because of the Cuban Adjustment Act of 1966. Under that law, Cuban immigrants who are not considered a threat to society are automatically granted permanent-resident status after being in the United States for one year. In 1988, an influential political organization, the Cuban-American National Foundation (CANF), entered into a special agreement with the U.S. government to handle Cuban immigration. The foundation, with headquarters in Miami, has screened, selected, and settled almost 8,000 *balseros*, the desperate refugees who flee Cuba on rafts, inner tubes, and anything else that floats. In 1991, 2,203 refugee rafters arrived in the United States. The foundation interviews the refugees, locates relatives, and arranges for transportation and jobs.

Anti-Castro cliches and news from Cuba dominate Miami's Spanish-language media. The lobbying arm of the CANF, the Cuban-American Foundation, has worked hard to tighten the economic screws on Castro. In Miami, "local political campaigns, even among non-Cubans, have at times become contests over who is more anticommunist, who has been a more vigorous supporter of Ronald Reagan, or who was more directly involved in the Bay of Pigs invasion."[2] Last year, the CANF promoted legislation that would cut aid to countries that buy Cuban sugar and penalize firms whose foreign subsidiaries trade with Cuba.

Planning for a post-Castro Cuba is well under way at the Cuban-American Foundation in Washington. Members have both an economic plan and a new constitution for Cuba, though there is no guarantee that they will take power when Castro falls. The best known of its members, Jorge Mas Canosa, a millionaire who plans to succeed Castro in post-socialist Cuba, sponsored the first trip by Boris Yeltsin to the United States in 1989. Mr. Yeltsin offered then to cut military aid to Cuba. Under pressure from the Bush administration in 1991, Gorbachev agreed to cut military aid to Cuba as a condition for U.S. economic assistance to the Soviets. Florida's exile community has since sped up preparations for the day when Fidel Castro falls.

Wall Street has joined in the odds-making.[3] Speculators bet that a new government will clear up old debts to attract new money. Having learned from experience with Mexican debt, they don't want to miss out on the rush. (In 1990, Mexican government bonds rocketed from $0.30 on the dollar to $0.57 once it agreed to swap its securities for new ones.) Some speculators have unearthed long-forgotten Cuban stocks and bonds that have not paid dividends or interest in years. The pre-1960 government debt, which Castro repudiated when he came into power, has become popular. One 1937 bond issue, listed on the New York Stock Exchange, doubled in price, from $0.20 on the dollar early in 1991 to $0.40 in October. There is no guarantee that Cuba will ever pay its debt, and Castro's surrender of power is far from certain.

Although influential Cuban-Americans want a tougher stance toward Castro, including an invasion, they won't get it unless President Bush needs a saber to rattle before the election. Moreover, the president could start listening to a new Cuban-American leadership that deemphasizes anti-Castro politics in favor of dialogue. Although hostility toward the Cuban government remains widespread, there is considerable sentiment for improved relations that would facilitate travel and communication between the two nations.

The U.S. demand that Moscow withdraw troops from Cuba bought time in negotiating aid to the Soviets. Bush will take no political risks with Cuba if he can avoid it. Thus major shifts in policy are liable to linger on the back burner.

## Aid

The Kremlin's decision to withdraw troops from Cuba was read as a blunt sign that the defeat of August's hard-line coup had decimated the ranks of Cuba's supporters in the Soviet government. The soldiers were proof of Soviet ideological commitment to Cuba. Now Moscow's relationship with Havana will change radically even if commercial exchanges continue.

New trade agreements with republics will be less favorable than the last Soviet one, itself substantially worse than the previous five-year agreement that ended in 1990. For Cuba, the military withdrawal represents another blow to people already faint from the collapse of Comecon trade and growing shortages of food and fuel. Castro has been preparing Cubans for another round of shortages. Cuba has a so-called zero-option in case the situation deteriorates further: food would be distributed in soup kitchens, gas for private use withdrawn, and the supply of electricity severely rationed.

There is no reason to prolong the burden of Castro's mistakes on innocent people. Once Cuba agrees to reform, the United States should be ready to help. Cuba will need assistance to deal with its disintegrating economy. Cuba's economy, built around subsidized sugar production for the Soviets, cannot be easily transformed into a competitive modern economy. Moreover, the government has accumulated a huge debt. Humanitarian aid could certainly help out in the transition to a healthier economy, without weakening economic reform.

The United States can also facilitate growth by developing a free trade agreement, like that under negotiation between the United States and Mexico, and by extending to Cuba the Caribbean Basin Initiative, which grants tax incentives for investment in the region.

A swift response to change in Cuba is essential to establish political support for a market economy. People learn only too quickly that capitalism can leave the weak, the old, and the poor in the dust. If the United States hopes to market some kinder, gentler version of capitalism, it had better move fast. The alternative is a return to the ugly corruption and inequality of the past, with resentment rekindling guerrilla movements.

Past U.S. policy has been an abomination, with missteps at nearly every turn. From the start, we put Castro in a box, giving him no option but to turn to the Soviets, despite the fuzzy mix of ideologies that influenced early events. The Bay of Pigs invasion and the economic embargo never succeeded in undermining Castro, and instead gave him plenty of leverage to blame most hardships on the United States. Charges of Yankee imperialism date back at least to 1853, when Jefferson Davis, later the U.S. Secretary of War, argued that to guarantee slavery, Cuba should be acquired, by negotiation if possible, by conquest if not.[4] Our policies have long left a bitter taste with Cubans. Can we do better?

A U. S. Agenda

U.S. policy toward Cuba should seek a constructive role. Debate should start now, beyond the Cuban-American community. Here is our guide to how the United States should proceed.

1. **Resist the temptation to overthrow Castro now.** Why turn down a golden opportunity? Remember that the United States must live with Cuba after Castro. Intervention will only enable the next generation to use the United States as a scapegoat for the consequences of bad policy.

2. **Remove travel restrictions and the trade embargo immediately.** Interaction is the best way to modernize Cuba and get rid of a rigid socialist mentality. Special quotas for Cuban sugar may be politically infeasible, but all other economic ties should be encouraged.

3. **Use Mexican diplomacy to bring Cuba home.** Both countries have engaged in a long, elusive search for independence from their northern neighbor. Mexico can mediate between Cuban pride and U.S. power.

4. **Arrange for Cuban Membership in the World Bank and the International Monetary Fund.** This is the best way to help the Cuban government phase in reforms and stabilization. Technical assistance, as with the Soviet Union, is badly

needed and can start immediately. These two organizations have the clout and resources to back a transition from socialism. No one needs a Cuban Reconstruction Bank and superfluous bureaucracy.

5. **Develop a strategy to make Cuba economically viable.** Cuba's task ahead requires implementation of a new institutional framework, strategies for economic diversification, sound fiscal and monetary policy, and sensitive handling of distributional issues. Only good economics can avoid a Soviet-style collapse and the dismantling of social stability.

6. **Urge Cuba to privatize.** With the assistance of the World Bank and the IMF, privatization can create opportunities for joint ventures between a new Cuban private sector and foreign firms. Cubans must learn fast to become the innovative capitalists the country needs to build a better future.

7. **Allocate $1 billion a year for the next five years for Cuba's reconstruction.** That is approximately 5 percent of Cuban gross national product, a Marshall Plan-sized commitment to peace and social progress. The United States must choose between constructive aid and uncontrolled immigration. It can avoid another Haiti.

We have argued throughout this book that Cuba must take steps toward change. In its own interest, the U.S. should turn from a policy of isolating Cuba to one of helping, as Cubans search for an acceptable path toward capitalism.

# Appendix A
## Chronology of Important Events

**1500s**   Spain colonizes Cuba.

**1898**   The United States intervenes in the Cuban War of Independence. Spain concedes defeat. The United States establishes a military government.

**1901**   The "Platt amendment" allowing U.S. intervention in Cuban affairs is incorporated in the new Cuban constitution, and U.S. troops leave Cuba.

**1906–1922**   U.S. forces occupy Cuba between 1906 and 1909, intervene in 1912, and are stationed in Cuba between 1917 and 1922.

**1933–1934**   The Machado dictatorship is overthrown. U.S. naval forces sail near Havana.

**1952**   Fulgencio Batista takes power by military coup.

**1953**   Fidel Castro leads attack on Moncada barracks.

**1959**   Revolutionary forces enter Havana. Agrarian reform law nationalizes one third of the arable land in Cuba.

**1960** Soviet Union signs trade agreement with Cuba. Eisenhower approves planning for Bay of Pigs invasion. U.S. oil companies refuse to refine Soviet crude oil at Cuban refineries; Cuba nationalizes refineries. Washington suspends Cuban sugar quota, blocking 80 percent of Cuban exports to United States. Soviet Union buys Cuban sugar. Cuba nationalizes $1 billion worth of private U.S. investment; Washington imposes trade embargo.

**1961** Washington breaks diplomatic relations with Cuba. CIA-sponsored invasion force of 1,200 exiles lands at Bay of Pigs and is defeated within seventy-two hours.

**1962** The Organization of American States (OAS) expels Cuba. Soviets send nuclear missiles to Cuba. Washington threatens to remove them. Soviets pull missiles out in exchange for U.S. pledge not to attack Cuba.

**1962–1968** The CIA organizes paramilitary attacks against Cuba and assassination plots against Cuban leaders.

**1964** OAS votes to require all members to cut diplomatic and trade relations with Cuba. Mexico refuses.

**1965** Boatlift from Camariorca brings 3,000 Cubans to the United States.

**1970** Washington warns Moscow to stop building nuclear submarine base at Cienfuegos, Cuba.

**1975** An OAS majority (including the United States) votes to lift diplomatic and economic sanctions against Cuba. Washington opts to retain its own trade embargo, but allows foreign subsidiaries of U.S. corporations to trade with

Cuba. Cuba sends combat troops to help Angola repulse an invasion by South African forces; eventually 30,000 troops are sent. U.S. President Gerald Ford says Cuban involvement in Angola precludes possibility of restoring relations and breaks off secret negotiations under way since 1974.

**1976** Bomb on Cubana airlines kills seventy-three people. Luis Posada Carriles, Cuban exile and former CIA employee, is arrested for the bombing in Venezuela.

**1977** Carter administration lifts ban on travel to Cuba. Cuban troops are sent to Ethiopia, derailing the process of normalizing relations.

**1978** Dialogue between members of the Cuban-American community and Cuban government leads to release of 3,600 political prisoners and agreements on travel and emigration.

**1979** Grenada restores diplomatic relations with Cuba, and subsequently establishes close political and economic ties. Revolutionary Nicaraguan government restores relations with Cuba. It then establishes political ties and receives military aid in war with U.S.-backed Contras.

**1980** Cuba announces that anyone wishing to leave can be picked up at port of Mariel. Over five months, 120,000 leave. Castro takes advantage of opportunity to send criminals and mental patients to the United States.

**1982** Reagan administration reimposes ban on travel to Cuba.

**1983** United States invades Grenada, where there are 636 Cuban construction workers and 43 military advisers.

**1984** Washington and Havana reach agreement under which Cuba receives 2,746 "excludables" who arrived during Mariel exodus, while United States permits immigration of up to 20,000 Cubans per year.

**1985** The United States begins to broadcast to Cuba over Radio Marti. Cuba suspends immigration agreement. Reagan administration bans travel by Cuban officials to the United States.

**1987** Eight Latin American nations call for Cuban readmission to OAS. Cuban-U.S. immigration agreement is restored. Cuban detainees in United States riot because they do not want to return to Cuba.

**1988** Angola agrees to send home all Cuban troops as part of a comprehensive Southern Africa peace settlement under negotiation.

**1989** Withdrawal from Angola begins. Castro opposes perestroika and glasnost.

**1990** Castro denounces reform movement sweeping Eastern Europe, pledges improvements to perfect communism in Cuba, and cracks down on human rights activists. The economic situation continues to deteriorate as Soviets cut subsidies and trade flows are reduced.

**1991** The Soviets decide to withdraw their troops from Cuba and end subsidies. Rumors surface that Spain has offered asylum to Castro.

# Appendix B
# Cuba's Political and Economic Structure

**Political Structure**

**Head of state:** President Fidel Castro Ruz

**Vice-president:** Raúl Castro Ruz

**Main political organization:** Partido Comunista de Cuba (PCC)

**Executive structure:** Council of Ministers, headed by the president

**National legislature:** The National Assembly of People's Power sits twice a year and consists of 481 members. Deputies are elected by the Municipal Assemblies of People's Power for periods of five years. In between the two sittings of the Assembly, the 31 member Council of the State takes over its function.

**Last national election:** April 1989
**Next election:** April 1994

**Local government:**  There are 14 provinces and 169 municipalities. Each municipality has an elected municipal assembly. Communist Party members propose the provincial and regional executive committees. The Party writes biographies for each candidate. Campaigning is prohibited.

**Legal system:**  The People's Supreme Court, which is accountable to the National Assembly, oversees a system of regional tribunals.

**Statistical Profile**

**Area:**  114,524 square kilometers (44,218 square miles, about the size of Pennsylvania)

**Population:**  11 million in 1990, growing at 0.9 percent per year

**Income per capita:**  Approximately U.S. $1,800 per year

**Life expectancy:**  75 years (the Central American and Caribbean average is  less than 70)

**Infant mortality:**  12 per 1,000 live births (the Central American and Caribbean average is above 70)

**Population per physician:**  530

**Literacy rate:**  95 percent of the population

**School attendance by age group (percentage):**
6 to 11:  100
12 to 17:  83
18 to 23:  30

**Real growth rate of global social product (percentage):**

1987: –3.5

1988:   2.1

1989:   2.0

1990: –1.5

**Average exchange rate:**   0.79 pesos per $ U.S.

**Origins of global social product as percent of total:**

Agriculture and forestry              15.9

Industry                              46.0

Construction                           9.3

Transport and communications           8.0

Commerce                              20.1

**Main exports:**   Sugar, seafood products, fruits, and tobacco

**Main imports:**   Petroleum products, food, chemicals, machinery, and transport equipment

**Main trade partners:**   In 1988, socialist countries bought 86 percent of total Cuban exports and sold 87 percent of total Cuban imports.

**Budget deficit as percent of global social product:**

1985:  0.9

1986:  0.7

1987:  2.4

1988:  4.4

1989:  5.2

Sources: Comité Estatal de Estadística, *Anuario estadístico de Cuba 1989*, Havana, 1991; World Bank, *World Development Report 1991*, Washington, D.C.: 1991; CEPAL, *Estudio económico de América Latina y el Caribe, 1989, Cuba*, United Nations, November 1990.

# Appendix C
## Statistical Data

**Table A.1**
Growth of per capita income in Cuba: Averages during the period 1969–1989 (percent per year)

| Source: | Official | Pérez-López | CIA | Tabares and Hidalgo | Zimbalist and Brundenius |
|---|---|---|---|---|---|
| Concept: | GSP | GDP | GNP | GDP | GDP |
| Units: | (real pesos) | (real pesos) | (real pesos) | (current dollars) | (dollars of 1980) |
| 1969–1975 | 9.7 | 3.9 | 0.9 | n.a. | 4.3 |
| 1976–1982 | 6.3 | 3.5 | n.a. | 6.1 | 5.4 |
| 1983–1985 | 4.5 | n.a. | n.a. | 0.8 | 4.5 |
| 1986–1989 | -1.1 | n.a. | n.a. | -2.2 | n.a. |

Source: Table A.4.

**Table A.2**
Cuban GDP per capita, in current pesos and $U.S., 1975–1989

| | Per capita GDP (pesos)[a] | Exchange rate (pesos/$U.S.)[b] | Per capita GDP ($U.S.)[a b] |
|---|---|---|---|
| 1975 | 1,113.7 | 0.83 | 1,343 |
| 1976 | 1,145.8 | 0.83 | 1,382 |
| 1977 | 1,158.3 | 0.76 | 1,526 |
| 1978 | 1,290.8 | 0.72 | 1,788 |
| 1979 | 1,313.7 | 0.72 | 1,817 |
| 1980 | 1,367.8 | 0.71 | 1,926 |
| 1981 | 1,589.8 | 0.78 | 2,038 |
| 1982 | 1,667.3 | 0.83 | 2,009 |
| 1983 | 1,766.8 | 0.86 | 2,054 |
| 1984 | 1,865.8 | 0.89 | 2,096 |
| 1985 | 1,893.3 | 0.92 | 2,058 |
| 1986 | 1,803.7 | 0.83 | 2,173 |
| 1987 | 1,755.3 | 1.00 | 1,755 |
| 1988 | 1,819.5 | 1.00 | 1,820 |
| 1989 | 1,837.4 | 1.00 | 1,837 |

a. Lourdes Tabares Neyra and Vilma Hidalgo de los Santos, "Una estimación de los principales agregados macroeconómicos de Cuba," Faculdad de Economía, Universidad de la Habana, unpublished manuscript, Dec.1990.

b. 1975–1979: *Pick's Currency Yearbook;* 1980–1989: Economic Commission for Latin America and the Caribbean, *Estudio económico de América Latina y el Caribe, 1989, Cuba,* Santiago: Naciones Unidas, Nov.1990, p.28.

**Table A.3**
Per capita product, Cuba, 1965–1989 (indices and U.S. dollars)

| Source: | Official | Pérez-López | Pérez-López | Brundenius | CIA | Zimbalist and Brundenius | Tabares and Hidalgo | Official |
|---|---|---|---|---|---|---|---|---|
| Concept: | GSP | GSP | GDP | GDP | GDP | GDP | GDP | GSP |
| Units: | Real pesos Index | Real pesos Index | Real pesos Index | Real pesos Index | Real pesos Index | Real dollars of 1980 | Current dollars | Current dollars |
| | a | b | c | d | e | f | g | h |
| 1965 | 50 | 76 | 73 | 73 | | 1,421 | | |
| 1966 | 50 | 80 | 77 | 72 | | 1,367 | | |
| 1967 | 54 | 89 | 86 | 74 | | 1,438 | | |
| 1968 | 55 | 81 | 81 | 78 | 100 | 1,482 | | |
| 1969 | 54 | 79 | 80 | 76 | 101 | 1,469 | | |
| 1970 | 62 | 76 | 77 | 76 | 104 | 1,564 | | |
| 1971 | 67 | 83 | 83 | 75 | 100 | 1,553 | | |
| 1972 | 77 | 88 | 87 | 82 | 98 | 1,616 | | |
| 1973 | 89 | 95 | 95 | 92 | 103 | 1,742 | | |
| 1974 | 100 | 100 | 100 | 100 | 104 | 1,841 | | |
| 1975 | 104 | 104 | 105 | 110 | 106 | 1,978 | 1,343 | |
| 1976 | 105 | 106 | 108 | 120 | | 2,049 | 1,382 | |
| 1977 | 124 | 111 | 113 | 130 | | 2,134 | 1,526 | |
| 1978 | 121 | 114 | 120 | 138 | | 2,281 | 1,788 | |
| 1979 | 126 | 118 | 123 | 141 | | 2,329 | 1,817 | |
| 1980 | 131 | 116 | 120 | 145 | | 2,325 | 1,926 | |
| 1981 | 151 | 122 | 130 | 158 | | 2,739 | 2,038 | |
| 1982 | 157 | 124 | 133 | | | 2,841 | 2,009 | |
| 1983 | 163 | | | | | 2,965 | 2,054 | |
| 1984 | 173 | | | | | 3,156 | 2,096 | 2,929 |
| 1985 | 179 | | | | | 3,245 | 2,058 | 2,902 |
| 1986 | 180 | | | | | | 2,178 | 3,132 |
| 1987 | 171 | | | | | | 1,755 | 2,481 |
| 1988 | 173 | | | | | | 1,820 | 2,530 |
| 1989 | 173 | | | | | | 1,837 | 2,558 |

Sources:

a From 1965 to 1982: *Anuario estadístico de Cuba, apud* Jorge F.Pérez-López, *Measuring Cuban Economic Performance*, Austin: University of Texas Press, 1987, p.118; from 1982 to 1989: Economic Commission for Latin American and the Caribbean, *Estudio económico de América Latina y el Caribe, 1989, Cuba*, Santiago: Naciones Unidas, Nov. 1990, p.11.

b. Pérez-López, *opus cit.*, p.117.

c. Pérez-López, idem.

d. Claes Brundenius, *Revolutionary Cuba: The Challenge of Growth with Equity*, Boulder: Westview Press, 1984, p.39.

e. Central Intelligence Agency, *The Cuban Economy: A Statistical Review, 1968-76*, ER 76-10708, Washington D.C., December 1976, p.2.

f. A. Zimbalist and C. Brundenius, *The Cuban Economy: Measurement and Analysis of Socialist Performance*, Baltimore: Johns Hopkins University Press, 1989, p.63.

g. Lourdes Tabares Neyra and Vilma Hidalgo de los Santos, "Una estimación de los principales agregados macroeconómicos de Cuba," Facultad de Economía, Universidad de la Habana, unpublished manuscript, Dec.1990, Appendix.

h. Calculated by dividing the official GSP measure in current pesos by the peso/dollar exchange rate. The GSP measure is reported in *Cuba Country Profile 1990-91*, London: The Economist Intelligence Unit, November 1990, p.11, and the exchange rate in Economic Commission for Latin American and the Caribbean, *Estudio económico de América Latina y el Caribe, 1989, Cuba*, Santiago: Naciones Unidas, Nov.1990, p.28.

**Table A.4**
Cuban per capita growth rates, 1966–1989 (percent per year)

| Source: | Official | Pérez-López | Pérez-López | Brundenius | CIA | Zimbalist and Brundenius | Tabares and Hidalgo | Official |
|---|---|---|---|---|---|---|---|---|
| Concept: | GSP | GSP | GDP | GDP | GDP | GDP | GDP | GDP |
| Units: | Real pesos | Real pesos | Real pesos | Real pesos | Real pesos | Real dollars | Current dollars | Current dollars |
| 1966 | 0.0 | 5.3 | 5.5 | -1.4 | | -3.9 | | |
| 1967 | 8.0 | 11.3 | 11.7 | 2.8 | | 5.2 | | |
| 1968 | 1.9 | -9.0 | -5.8 | 5.4 | | 3.1 | | |
| 1969 | -1.8 | -2.5 | -1.2 | -2.6 | 0.5 | -0.9 | | |
| 1970 | 14.8 | -3.8 | -3.8 | 0.0 | 3.7 | 6.5 | | |
| 1971 | 8.1 | 9.2 | 7.8 | -1.3 | -4.0 | -0.7 | | |
| 1972 | 14.9 | 6.0 | 4.8 | 9.3 | -1.8 | 4.1 | | |
| 1973 | 15.6 | 8.0 | 9.2 | 12.2 | 5.1 | 7.8 | | |
| 1974 | 12.4 | 5.3 | 5.3 | 8.7 | 0.7 | 5.7 | | |
| 1975 | 4.0 | 4.0 | 5.0 | 10.0 | 2.0 | 7.5 | | |
| 1976 | 0.9 | 1.9 | 2.9 | 9.1 | | 3.6 | 2.9 | |
| 1977 | 18.1 | 4.7 | 4.6 | 8.3 | | 4.2 | 10.4 | |
| 1978 | -2.4 | 2.7 | 6.2 | 6.2 | | 6.9 | 17.2 | |
| 1979 | 4.1 | 3.5 | 2.5 | 2.2 | | 2.1 | 1.6 | |
| 1980 | 4.0 | -1.7 | -2.4 | 2.8 | | -0.2 | 6.0 | |
| 1981 | 15.3 | 5.2 | 8.3 | 9.0 | | 17.8 | 5.8 | |
| 1982 | 4.0 | 1.6 | 2.3 | | | 3.7 | -1.4 | |
| 1983 | 3.9 | | | | | 4.4 | 2.3 | |
| 1984 | 6.2 | | | | | 6.4 | 2.0 | |
| 1985 | 3.5 | | | | | 2.8 | -1.8 | -0.9 |
| 1986 | 0.2 | | | | | | 5.6 | 8.0 |
| 1987 | -4.8 | | | | | | -19.2 | -20.8 |
| 1988 | 1.4 | | | | | | 3.7 | 2.0 |
| 1989 | 0.0 | | | | | | 1.0 | 1.1 |

Source: Table A.3.

**Table A.5**
Cuban peso/dollar exchange rate, 1970–1990

| Year | Official rate | Black market rate |
|------|---------------|-------------------|
| 1970 | 1.00 | 7.00 |
| 1971 | 0.92 | 9.70 |
| 1972 | 0.92 | 9.00 |
| 1973 | 0.82 | 9.75 |
| 1974 | 0.83 | 9.25 |
| 1975 | 0.83 | 8.60 |
| 1976 | 0.83 | 10.40 |
| 1977 | 0.76 | 11.74 |
| 1978 | 0.72 | 13.60 |
| 1979 | 0.72 | 13.00 |
| 1980 | 0.71 | 18.00 |
| 1981 | 0.78 | 22.00 |
| 1982 | 0.83 | 19.00 |
| 1983 | 0.86 | 18.50 |
| 1984 | 0.89 | 22.00 |
| 1985 | 0.92 | 25.00 |
| 1986 | 0.83 | 29.00 |
| 1987 | 1.00 | 30.00 |
| 1988 | 1.00 | 35.00 |

Sources: Economic Commission for Latin America and the Caribbean (CEPAL), *Cuba, Estudio económico de América Latina y el Caribe, 1989,* United Nations, November 1990; and *Pick's Currency Yearbook,* 1990.

# Notes

## Preface

1. Mark Falcoff, "The Day Castro Dies," *The International Economy*, September/October 1991, p. 53.

2. Susan Kaufman Purcell, "Is Cuba Changing?" *The National Interest*, no. 14, Winter 1988/89, pp. 43–53.

3. Andrew Zimbalist, "Introduction," in Andrew Zimbalist, ed., *Cuba's Socialist Economy towards the 1990s*, Boulder, CO: Lynne Rienner Publishers, 1987, p. 1.

4. Juan Luis Cebrian, quoted by Jacobo Timerman, *Cuba, A Journey*, New York: Alfred Knopf, 1990, pp. 11–12.

## Chapter 1

1. Following the economic reforms of 1978 in China, inequality increased as the economy shifted toward more market-oriented policies. In particular, rural poverty decreased while urban poverty increased. Even in an economy that remains highly centralized, there is a trade-off between policies that promote equality (even though at a lower income level) and policies that raise monetary incomes but create greater income variability and vulnerability. (Etishm Ahmad and Yan Wang, "Inequality and Poverty in China: Institutional Change and Public Policy," *The World Bank Economic Review*, 5(2), May 1991, pp. 231–258).

2. Global social product (GSP) is a measure of the total flow of goods produced by the economy over a specified time period, normally a year.

3. *Financial Times*, Sept. 14, 1991.

4. A local drink consisting of rum, sugar, lime, seltzer, and mint leaves.

## Chapter 2

1. Gerardo Machado was elected president in 1924. After silencing his opposition through deportation and assassination, he was re-elected in 1928. He responded to the 1930s crisis with repression and terror.

2. Harvey Kline, "Cuba: The Politics of Socialist Revolution," in Howard Wiarda and Harvey Kline, ed., *Latin American Politics and Development*, Boulder, CO: Westview Press, 1985.

3. Edward González, *Cuba Under Castro: The Limits of Charisma*, Boston: Houghton Mifflin, 1974.

4. S. Collier, H. Blakemore, and T. Skidmore, *Cambridge Encyclopedia of Latin America*, Cambridge: Cambridge University Press, 1985, p. 278.

5. Quoted by Hugh Thomas in *Cuba: The Pursuit of Freedom*, New York: Harper and Row Publishers, 1971, p. 977.

6. Quoted by Hugh Thomas in *Cuba: The Pursuit of Freedom*, New York: Harper and Row Publishers, 1971, p. 1022.

7. With the exception of a brief period in 1980–82, private farmers have operated under difficult conditions: high state procurement quotas at low prices, delays in state payments, and restrictions on the sale of surplus. Nonetheless, they have played a prominent role in production. Between 1976 and 1980, private farms produced: 89 percent of total coffee and cacao, 82 percent of corn, 78 percent of tobacco, 64 percent of beans, 40 percent of fruits, 62 percent of green vegetables, and 18 percent of sugarcane.

8. Archibald Ritter, *The Economic Development of Revolutionary Cuba*, New York, Praeger Press, 1974, p. 146 and p. 188.

9. Estimates by the Comisión Económica para América Latina (CEPAL) cited in Cole Blasier, *The Giant's Rival: The U.S.S.R. and Latin America*, Pittsburgh: University of Pittsburgh Press, 1983, p. 119.

10. A. Zimbalist and C. Brundenius, *The Cuban Economy: Measurement and Analysis of Socialist Performance*, Baltimore: Johns Hopkins University Press, 1989, p. 78.

11. More detailed data are provided in tables A.1–A.4 in appendix C.

12. These numbers appeared in the *New York Times*, September 12, 1991. These estimates were based on data from the CIA and the International Institute for Strategic Studies.

13. *Financial Times*, September 15, 1991.

## Chapter 3

1. Bill Keller, from Moscow, for the *New York Times*, March 7, 1991.

2. Applications for visas to visit the United States also increased as restrictions were eased. Previously the Cuban government allowed only men over 65 years of age and women over 60 to leave. In March 1990, the thresholds were lowered to 35 for men and 30 for women.

3. Some saw the intellectual crisis earlier than others. Felipe Pazos, a collaborator of Castro in the struggle against Batista and president of the Central Bank after the revolution, left the country in 1960. He wrote in 1961: "The Cuban revolution has ceased to be the proof of rationality and efficiency of the socialist system. It demonstrates the failure of totalitarian socialism." (*El Trimestre Económico* n. 111, 1962).

4. Economic Commission for Latin America and the Caribbean, *Cuba, 1989*, Santiago: United Nations, Nov. 1990.

5. José Luis Rodríguez, "La economía Cubana ante un mundo cambiante," Cuba: CIEM, Havana, May 1991.

## Chapter 4

1. External resources for Nicaragua's stabilization program available from April, 1991 on, amounted to $464 million. The two major donors were the United States ($264 million) and Taiwan ($60 million), according to a report by the Ministério de Cooperación Externa (April 1991).

2. Between 1973 and 1974, 360 companies (with an aggregate book value of $1 billion) were returned to their previous owners. Between 1975 and 1980, ninety companies and sixteen banks were sold through public auctions yielding a total of $1 billion.

3. Interferons inhibit life-threatening viral infections. All vertebrate animals produce their own particular interferons. They are also produced by cells cultured outside the body. Applications of interferon include the treatment of shingles, hepatitis B, and benign tumors of the skin, throat, and genital area.

## Chapter 5

1. The State Department estimates that in 1990 Cuba received about $3.5 billion in economic aid and about $1 billion in military aid from the Soviet Union. It is unlikely that new agreements with Soviet republics will match the special one-year agreement under which the Soviet Union supplied Cuba with 8 million tons of crude oil and 2 million tons of derivatives, at $20 a barrel, and the Cubans exported 4 million tons of sugar at 24 cents a pound, substantially above the international price, which is currently at 9 cents.

2. *Latin American Regional Reports, Caribbean*, London: November 8, 1990, p. 2.

3. See Olivier Blanchard et. al., *Reform in Eastern Europe*, Cambridge, MA: MIT Press, 1991.

4. The Cuban peso was linked at par to the U.S. dollar in November 1914, and to the pound sterling in 1961. Since June 1976, it is on a controlled, floating basis (see table A.5 in the statistical appendix). Effective commercial selling rates are based on the official peso plus import taxes of 30, 40, 60, 80, and 100 percent, depending on how

essential the good is considered. The tourist rate has reflected a premium of 30–50 percent over the base rate for payment of travel expenses in U.S. dollars. Foreign trade is a state monopoly. Cuban residents cannot import or export national banknotes or own foreign currency, nor can they maintain bank balances abroad. The black market rate (table A.5 in the statistical appendix) results from unauthorized dealings of foreign currency or unlicensed transfers abroad.

5. Hugh Bradenkamp, "Reforming the Soviet Economy," *Finance and Development*, June 1991, pp. 18–21.

6. The Mexican Institutional Revolutionary Party (PRI) is a huge, well-organized party that dominates the electoral process and provides mass support for the national and local governments.

7. In 1990, a Harris poll reported that 50 percent of respondents opposed economic aid to foreign countries, compared to 36 percent four years earlier (*Time*, May 14, 1990, p. 29).

8. Although Cuba has not published the data on its foreign debt, the Soviet Union and the Eastern European countries have claimed that in November 1989, the Cuban debt was equivalent to $17 billion to the Soviet Union and $1.5 billion to Eastern European countries. These numbers were not confirmed by Cuba. Cuba reports 6 billion pesos as its debt in convertible currency at the end of 1989.

## Chapter 6

1. *Wall Street Journal*, June 4, 1991.

2. Lisandro Pérez, ed., "The 1990s: Cuban Miami at the Crossroads," *Cuban Studies*, 20, University of Pittsburgh Press, 1990, p.21.

3. *The New York Times*, October 6, 1991.

4. Hugh Thomas, *Cuba: The Pusuit of Freedom*, New York: Harper and Row, 1971, p. 219.

# Bibliography

Abouchar, Alan. 1986. "The Treatment of Intermediate Goods in Cuban National Income Accounts: Parallels and Differences with Soviet Methodology." *Comparative Economic Studies* 28, no. 2 (Summer), pp. 37–48.

Accolla, Peter. 1989. "Privatization in Latin America." *Foreign Labor Trends*, U.S. Department of Labor.

Alvárez González, Elena. 1991. "Algunos efectos en la economía Cubana de los cambios en la conyuntura internacional." Havana: Instituto de Investigaciones Económicas, mimeo, June.

Bekarevich, Anatoli, and Kalev Keino. 1986. "Cuba: economía, planificación, gestión." In Academia de Ciencias de la URSS, *Cuba: 25 años de construcción del socialismo*. Moscow: Redacción Ciencias Sociales Contemporáneas.

Blanchard, Olivier et al. 1991. *Reform in Eastern Europe*. Cambridge, MA: MIT Press.

Boodhoo, Ken I. 1989. "Growth and Development: Meeting Basic Needs in Cuba and the Caribbean." *Caribbean Affairs* 2, no. 3 (July–Sept.), pp. 22–41.

Brenner, Philip. 1990. "Cuba and the Missile Crisis." *Journal of Latin American Studies* 22 (1), pp. 115–142.

Brundenius, Claes. 1981. "Growth with Equity: The Cuban Experience (1959–1980)." *World Development* 9, nos. 11–12 (Nov.–Dec.), pp. 1083–1107.

Brundenius, Claes. 1984. *Revolutionary Cuba: The Challenge of Economic Growth with Equity*. Boulder, CO: Westview.

Brundenius, Claes, and Mats Lundahl, eds. 1982. *Development Strategies and Basic Needs in Latin America: Challenges for the 1980s*. Boulder, CO: Westview.

Brundenius, Claes, and Andrew Zimbalist. 1985a. "Recent Studies on Cuban Economic Growth: A Review." *Comparative Economic Studies* 27, no. 1 (Spring), pp. 21–45.

Brundenius, Claes, and Andrew Zimbalist. 1985b. "Cuban Economic Growth One More Time: A Response to 'Imbroglios.'" *Comparative Economic Studies* 27, no. 3 (Fall), pp. 115–131.

Brundenius, Claes, and Andrew Zimbalist. 1985c. "Cuban Growth: A Final Word." *Comparative Economic Studies* 27, no. 4 (Winter), pp. 83–84.

Brundenius, Claes, and Andrew Zimbalist. 1988. "Cubanology and Economic Performance." In *Cuban Political Economy: Controversies in Cubanology*, edited by Andrew Zimbalist. Boulder, CO: Westview.

Cardoso, Eliana. 1991. "Privatization Fever in Latin America." *Challenge* (September/October).

Castro, Fidel. 1987. *Por el camino correcto*. Havana: Editora Política.

Castro, Fidel. 1988. *La revolución Cubana: una proeza extraordinaria*. Havana: Editora Política.

Collier, S., H. Blakemore, and T. Skidmore. 1985. *Cambridge Encyclopedia of Latin America*. Cambridge: Cambridge University Press.

Comité Estatal de Estadísticas. 1991. *Anuario estadístico de Cuba 1989*. Havana: Comité Estatal de Estadísticas.

Costa Santana, José. 1982. *Teoría y práctica de los mecanismos de dirección de la economía en Cuba*. Havana: Editorial de Ciencias Sociales.

Cuban American National Foundation. 1989. *The Cuban Revolution at Thirty*, Proceedings from the Conference Sponsored by the Cuban American National Foundation, Washington, D. C., January 10.

De Walle, Nicolas Van. 1989. "Privatization in Developing Countries: A Review of the Issues." *World Development* 17(5), pp. 601–615.

Díaz-Briquets, Sergio. 1988. "Regional Differences in Development and Living Standards in Revolutionary Cuba." *Cuban Studies* 18, pp. 45–63.

Díaz-Vázquez, Julio A. 1981. "Cuba: integración económica socialista y especialización de la producción." *Economía y desarrollo* 63 (July–Aug.), pp. 133–165.

Domínguez, Jorge. 1978. *Cuba: Order and Revolution.* Cambridge, MA: Belknap.

Domínguez, Jorge. 1983. "Cuba's Relation with Caribbean and Central American Countries." *Cuban Studies* 13 (2).

Domínguez, Jorge. 1988. "Cuba in the International Arena." *Latin American Research Review* 23 (1).

Domínguez, Jorge. 1989. To *Make a World Safe for Revolution: Cuba's Foreign Policy.* Cambridge, MA: Harvard University Press.

Dornbusch, Rudiger. 1991. *Priorities of Economic Reform in Eastern Europe and the Soviet Union.* Occasional Paper no. 5. London: Center for Economic Policy Research.

Echevarría Salvat, Oscar A. 1971. *La agricultura Cubana, 1934–1966.* Miami, FL: Ediciones Universal.

Eckstein, Susan. 1986. "The Impact of the Cuban Revolution: A Comparative Perspective." *Comparative Studies in Society and History* 28, no. 3 (July), pp. 502–534.

Economic Commission for Latin America and the Caribbean (CEPAL). 1990. *Cuba, estudio económico de América Latina y el Caribe, 1989.* United Nations, November.

Economist Intelligence Unit. 1991. *Cuba Country Profile 1990–91.* London: The Economist.

Feinsilver, Julie M. n.d. "Will Cuba's Wonder Drugs Lead to Political and Economic Wonders? Capitalizing on Biotechnology and Medical Exports." *Cuban Studies*, forthcoming.

Fernández Arner, Agustín, and Lillian Pla García. 1982. "El comercio exterior y la construcción del socialismo en Cuba." *Economía y desarrollo* 90 (Jan.–Feb.), pp. 39–49.

Fernández-Rubio Legra, Angel. 1985. *El proceso de institucionalización de la revolución Cubana.* Havana: Editorial de Ciencias Sociales.

Fitzgerald, Frank. 1989. "The Reform of the Cuban Economy, 1976–86: Organizations, Incentives and Patterns of Behavior." *Journal of Latin American Studies* 21 (2), pp. 283–310.

García Marrero, Agustín, and Antonio Morales Pita. 1987. "El desarrollo de los complejos agroindustriales azucareros en las condiciones de la república de Cuba." *Economía y desarrollo* 96 (Jan.–Feb.), pp. 60–79.

Geyer, Georgie Anne. 1991. *Guerilla Prince: The Untold Story of Fidel Castro.* Boston: Little Brown.

Glade, William, ed. 1991. *Privatization of Public Enterprises in Latin America,* International Center for Economic Growth. San Francisco: ICS Press.

González, Edward. 1974. *Cuba Under Castro: The Limits of Charisma.* Boston: Houghton Mifflin.

Goure, Leon, and Julian Winkle. 1972. "Cuba's New Dependency." *Problems of Communism* 21, no. 2 (Mar.–April), pp. 68–79.

Grupo Cubano de Investigaciones Económicas. 1963. *Un estudio sobre Cuba.* Coral Gables, FL: University of Miami Press.

Gunn, G. 1990. "Will Castro Fall?" *Foreign Policy* 79 (Summer).

Halebsky, Sandor, and John Kirk, eds. 1990. *Transformation and Struggle: Cuba Faces the 1990s.* New York: Praeger.

Hanke, Steve H. 1987. *Privatization and Development.* San Francisco, CA: Institute for Development Studies.

Hinds, Manuel. 1990. "Issues in the Introduction of Market Forces in Eastern European Socialist Economies," Working Paper. Washington, D.C.: World Bank.

Ibáñez Morales, Jesús R. 1988. "Las cuentas nacionales de Cuba, algo más que una conversión del SBEN al SCN." *Revista estadística* 10, no. 23 (Apr.), pp. 51–72.

ILPES (Instituto Latinomericano y del Caribe de Planificación Económica y Social). 1988. "El sistema de dirección y planificación de la economía Cubana." *Cuadernos del ILPES* 33. Santiago, Chile: United Nations.

Inter-American Development Bank. 1991. *Economic and Social Progress in Latin America: 1990 Report*. Washington, D.C.: Inter-American Development Bank.

Joglekar, Gitanjali, and Andrew Zimbalist. 1989. "Dollar GDP per Capita in Cuba." *Journal of Comparative Economics* 13, pp. 85–114.

Jorge, Antonio. 1983. "How Exportable Is the Cuban Model? Culture Contact in a Modern Context." In *The New Cuban Presence in the Caribbean*, edited by Barry Levine. Boulder, CO: Westview.

Jorge, Antonio, and Jaime Suchlicki, eds. 1989. *The Cuban Economy: Dependency and Development*. Miami: Institute of International Studies.

*Journal of Communist Studies*. 1989. Special Issue on Cuba After Thirty Years: Rectification and the Revolution 5 (4).

Kline, Harvey. 1978. "Fidel Castro and the Cuban Revolution." In *Governments and Leaders*, edited by Edward Feit. Boston: Houghton Mifflin.

Kline, Harvey. 1985. "Cuba: The Politics of Socialist Revolution." In *Latin American Politics and Development*, edited by Howard Wiarda and Harvey Kline. Boulder, CO: Westview.

*Latin Finance*. 1991. Supplement on Privatization in Latin America (March).

Lecaillon, Jacques et al. 1984. *Income Distribution and Economic Development: An Analytical Survey*. Geneva: International Labor Office.

Leogrande, William M. 1979. "Cuban Dependency: A Comparison of Pre-Revolutionary and Post-Revolutionary International Economic Relations." *Cuban Studies/Estudios Cubanos* 9, no. 2 (July), pp. 1–28.

Luxenburg, Norman. 1984. "Social Conditions Before and After the Revolution." In *Cuban Communism*, edited by Irving Louis Horowitz, fifth ed. New Brunswick, N.J.: Transaction.

Luzón, José L. 1988. "Housing in Socialist Cuba: An Analysis Using Cuban Censuses of Population and Housing." *Cuban Studies* 18, pp. 65–83.

Macdonald, Scott B., and F. Joseph Demetrius. 1986. "The Caribbean Sugar Crisis: Consequences and Challenges." *Journal of Inter-American Studies and World Affairs* 28, no.1 (Spring), pp. 35–58.

Marrero, Levi. 1987. *Cuba en la década de 1950: un país en desarrollo.* San Juan, Puerto Rico: Ediciones Capiro.

Martínez Carrera, Ramón. 1988. "Reflexiones sobre el trabajo de series cronológicas de la estadística económica en Cuba." *Revista estadística* 10, no. 24 (Aug.), pp. 59–91.

Martínez Salsamendi, Carlos. 1984. "El papel de Cuba en el tercer mundo; America Central, el Caribe y Africa." In *Cuba y Estados Unidos: un debate para la convivencia,* edited by Juan Gabriel Tokatlian. Buenos Aires: Grupo Impresor Latinoamericano.

Mesa-Lago, Carmelo. 1969. "Availability and Reliability of Statistics in Socialist Cuba." *Latin American Research Review* 4, no. 1 (Winter), pp. 59–91; and 4, no. 2 (Summer), pp. 47–81.

Mesa-Lago, Carmelo. 1971. "Economic Policies and Growth." In *Revolutionary Change in Cuba,* edited by Carmelo Mesa-Lago. Pittsburgh, PA: University of Pittsburgh Press.

Mesa-Lago, Carmelo. 1981. *The Economy of Socialist Cuba: A Two Decade Appraisal.* Albuquerque: University of New Mexico Press.

Mesa-Lago, Carmelo. 1986. "Cuba's Centrally Planned Economy: An Equity Trade-Off for Growth." In *Latin American Political Economy:Financial Crisis and Political Change,* edited by Jonathan Hartlyn and Samuel A. Morley. Boulder, CO: Westview.

Mesa-Lago, Carmelo. 1988. "The Cuban Economy in the 1980s: The Return of Ideology." In *Socialist Cuba, Past Interpretations and Future Challenges,* edited by Sergio Roca, pp. 59–100.

Mesa-Lago, Carmelo. 1989. "Cuba's Economic Counter-Reform: Causes, Policies and Effects." *Journal of Communist Studies.* Special Issue on Cuba After Thirty Years: Rectification and the Revolution 5 (4), pp. 98–139.

Mesa-Lago, Carmelo, and Sergio Díaz-Briquets. 1983. "Estrategias differentes, países similares: las consecuencias para el crecimiento y la equidad en Costa Rica y Cuba." *Anuario de estudios Centroamericanos* 14, nos. 1–2; 5–23.

Mesa-Lago, Carmelo, and Fernando Gil. 1989. "Soviet Economic Relations with Cuba." In *The USSR and Latin America: A Developing Relationship*, edited by Eusebio Mujal-León. Winchester, MA: Unwin Hyman.

Mesa-Lago, Carmelo, and Jorge Pérez-López. 1985a. "Estimating Cuban Gross Domestic Product per Capita in Dollars Using Physical Indicators." *Social Indicators Research* 16, pp. 275–300.

Mesa-Lago, Carmelo, and Jorge Pérez-López. 1985b. "A Study of Cuba's Material Product System, Its Conversion to the System of National Accounts, and Estimation of Gross Domestic Product per Capita and Growth Rates." World Bank Staff Working Paper no. 770. Washington, D.C.: World Bank.

Mesa-Lago, Carmelo, and Jorge Pérez-López. 1985c. "Imbroglios on the Cuban Economy: A Reply to Brundenius and Zimbalist." *Comparative Economic Studies* 27, no. 1 (Spring), pp. 21–45.

Mesa-Lago, Carmelo, and Jorge Pérez-López. 1985d. "The Endless Cuban Economic Saga: A Terminal Rebuttal." *Comparative Economic Studies* 27, no. 4 (Winter), pp. 67–82.

Mesa-Lago, Carmelo, and Luc Zephirin. 1971. "Central Planning." In *Revolutionary Change in Cuba*, edited by Carmelo Mesa-Lago. Pittsburgh, PA: University of Pittsburgh Press.

Mina, Gianni. 1981. *Habla Fidel*. Madrid: Mondadori España.

Moncarz, Raúl. 1989. "The Economics of Labor in Cuba: Factors Affecting Labor Productivity." In Jorge and Suchlicki, pp. 47–66.

O'Connor, James. 1970. *The Origins of Socialism in Cuba*. Ithaca, N.Y.: Cornell University Press.

Packenham, Robert A. 1986. "Capitalist Dependency and Socialist Dependency: The Case of Cuba." *Journal of Inter-American Studies and World Affairs* 28, no. 1 (Spring), pp. 59–92.

Pérez, Lisandro, ed. 1990. "The 1990s: Cuban Miami at the Crossroads." *Cuban Studies* 20.

Pérez-López, Jorge F. 1977. "An Index of Cuban Industrial Output, 1930–1958." In *Quantitative Latin American Studies: Methods and Findings*, edited by James W. Wilkie and Kenneth Ruddle. Los Angeles: Latin American Center, University of California.

Pérez-López, Jorge F. 1986a. "The Economics of Cuban Joint Ventures." *Cuban Studies* 16, pp. 181–207.

Pérez-López, Jorge F. 1986b. "Real Economic Growth in Cuba, 1965–1982." *Journal of Developing Areas* 20 (Jan.), pp. 151–172.

Pérez-López, Jorge F. 1987a. "Cuban Oil Reexports: Significance and Prospects." *The Energy Journal* 8, no. 1, pp. 1–16.

Pérez-López, Jorge F. 1987b. *Measuring Cuban Economic Performance.* Austin: University of Texas Press.

Pérez-López, Jorge F. 1987c. *Sugar and the Cuban Economy: An Assessment.* Coral Gables, FL: Research Institute for Cuban Studies, University of Miami.

Pérez-López, Jorge F. 1988a. "Cuban Hard-Currency Trade and Oil Reexports." In *Socialist Cuba: Past Interpretations and Future Challenges*, edited by Sergio G. Roca. Boulder, CO: Westview.

Pérez-López, Jorge F. 1988b. "Cuban-Soviet Sugar Trade: Price and Subsidy Issues." *Bulletin of Latin American Research* 7, no. 1, pp. 123–147.

Pérez-López, Jorge F. 1989. "Sugar and Structural Change in the Cuban Economy." *World Development* 17, no. 10 (Oct.), pp. 1627–1646.

Pérez-Stable, Marifeli. 1991. "The Field of Cuban Studies." *Latin American Research Review* 26 (1), pp. 339–350.

Pino-Santos, Oscar, and Osvaldo Martínez. 1979. *Relaciones económicas de Cuba con los países miembros del consejo de ayuda mutua económica (CAME).* Santiago, Chile: CEPAL.

Pollitt, Brian. 1967. "Estudios acerca del nivel de vida rural en la Cuba prerevolucionaria: un análisis crítico." *Teoría y práctica* 42–43 (Nov.–Dec.), pp. 32-50.

Purcell, Susan. 1988. "Is Cuba Changing?" *The National Interest* 14 (Winter), pp. 43–53.

Purcell, Susan. 1990. "Cuba's Cloudy Future." *Foreign Affairs* (Summer), pp. 113–130.

Radell, Willard W. 1983. "Cuban-Soviet Sugar Trade, 1960–1976: How Large Was the Subsidy?" *Journal of Developing Areas* 17, no.3 (Apr.), pp. 365–382.

Ritter, Archibald R. M. 1979. "The Transferability of Cuba's Revolutionary Development Model." In *Cuba in the World*, edited by Cole Blasier and Carmelo Mesa-Lago. Pittsburgh, PA: University of Pittsburgh Press.

Ritter, A. 1990. "The Cuban Economy in the 1990s: External Challenges and Policy Imperatives." *Journal of Inter-American Studies and World Affairs* 32, no. 3 (Fall).

Roca, Sergio G. 1984. "Rural Public Services in Socialist Cuba." In *Rural Public Services: International Comparisons*, edited by Richard E. Lonsdale and Gyorgy Enyedi. Boulder, CO: Westview.

Roca, Sergio G. 1986. "State Enterprises in Cuba under the System of Planning and Management (SDPE)." *Cuban Studies* 16, pp. 153–179.

Roca, Sergio G. 1987. "Planners in Wonderland: A Reply to Zimbalist." *Cuban Studies* 17, pp. 167–172.

Roca, Sergio G. 1988. "Cuban Planning: A Rebuttal to Zimbalist." *Cuban Studies* 18, pp. 167–168.

Roca, Sergio G., ed. 1988. *Socialist Cuba: Past Interpretations and Future Challenges*. Boulder, CO: Westview.

Roca, Sergio G., and Roberto E. Hernández. 1972. "Structural Economic Problems." In *Cuba, Castro, and Revolution*, edited by Jaime Suchlicki. Coral Gables, FL: University of Miami Press.

Rodríguez, José Luis. 1982. "La economía Cubana entre 1976 y 1980: resultados y perspectivas." *Economía y desarrollo* 66 (Jan.–Feb.), pp. 108–149.

Rodríguez, José Luis. 1984. "Un enfoque burgués del sector externo de la economía Cubana." *Cuba socialista* 5, no. l (Mar.–Apr), pp. 78–104.

Rodríguez, José Luis. 1986. "Las relaciones económicas Cuba-URSS, 1960–1985." *Temas de economía mundial* 17, pp. 9–33.

Rodríguez, José Luis. 1988. *Crítica a nuestros críticos.* Havana: Editorial de Ciencias Sociales.

Rodríguez, José Luis, and George Carriazo Morena. 1987. *Eradicación de la pobreza en Cuba.* Havana: Editorial de Ciencias Sociales.

Salazar-Carrillo, Jorge. 1989. "The National Economic Accounting System of Cuba: Notes on Its Evolution and Meaning." In Jorge and Suchlicki, editors, pp. 35–45.

Sanguinetty, Jorge A. 1989. "Cuban and Latin American Economics: Doctrine and Praxis." In *Cuba: The International Dimension,* edited by Georges Fauriol and Eva Loser. New Brunswick, N.J.: Transaction.

Seers, Dudley, ed. 1964. *Cuba: The Economic and Social Revolution.* Chapel Hill: University of North Carolina Press.

Sondrol, Paul. 1991. "Totalitarian and Authoritarian Dictators: A Comparison of Fidel Castro and Alfredo Stroessner." *Journal of Latin American Studies* 23, no. 3 (October), pp. 599–620.

Tabares Neyra, Lourdes, and Vilma Hidalgo de los Santos. 1990. "Una estimación de los principales agregados macroeconómicos de Cuba." Facultad de Economía, Universidad de la Habana, unpublished manuscript.

Thomas, Hugh. 1971. *Cuba, The Pursuit of Freedom.* New York: Harper and Row.

Turits, Richard. 1987. "Trade, Debt, and the Cuban Economy." *World Development* 15, no. 1 (Jan.), pp. 163–180.

Uhlig, Mark. 1991. "Latin America: The Frustrations of Success." *Foreign Affairs* 70 (1), pp. 103–119.

United Nations. 1990, 1991. *Human Development Report 1990* and *1991.* New York: Oxford University Press.

U.S. Central Intelligence Agency. 1976. *The Cuban Economy: A Statistical Review, 1968–1976.* Doc. no. ER78-10708, Washington, D.C.

U.S. Central Intelligence Agency. 1981. *The Cuban Economy: A Statistical Review.* Doc. no. ER81-10052. Washington, D.C.

U.S. Central Intelligence Agency. 1984. *The Cuban Economy: A Statistical Review*. Doc. no. ALA84-10052. Washington, D.C.

Valdés, María Teresa. 1984. "La evolución de la producción azucarera en Cuba y su papel en las relaciones económicas externas." *Temas de economía mundial* 10, pp. 117–149.

Vázquez, José. 1981. "Desarrollo azucarero." *Cuba internacional* (July), pp. 38–43.

Williamson, John. 1990. *The Progress of Reform in Latin America*. Washington, D.C.: Institute for International Economics.

World Bank. 1981, 1990, 1991. *World Development Report 1981, 1990, and 1991*. New York: Oxford University Press.

Zimbalist, Andrew. 1982. "Soviet Aid, U.S. Blockade, and the Cuban Economy." *ACES Bulletin* 24, no. 4 (Winter), pp. 137–146.

Zimbalist, Andrew. 1985. "Cuban Economic Planning: Organization and Performance." In *Cuba: Twenty-Five Years of Revolution, 1959–1984*, edited by Sandor Halebsky and John M. Kirk. New York: Praeger.

Zimbalist, Andrew. 1987a. "Cuban Industrial Growth, 1965–1984." *World Development* 15, no. 1 (Jan.), pp. 83–93.

Zimbalist, Andrew. 1987b. "Analyzing Cuban Planning: A Response to Roca." *Cuban Studies*, pp. 159–165.

Zimbalist, Andrew, ed. 1987c. *Cuba's Socialist Economy Toward the 1990s*. Boulder, CO: Lynne Rienner.

Zimbalist, Andrew. 1988a. "Cuba's External Economy: Reflections on Export Dependence, Soviet Aid, and Foreign Debt." *Comparative Economic Studies* 30, no.2 (Summer), pp. 21–46.

Zimbalist, Andrew. 1988b. "Cuban Planning: A Rejoinder to Roca." *Cuban Studies* 18, pp. 165–166.

Zimbalist, Andrew. 1988c. "Cuba's Statistical and Price Systems: Interpretation and Reliability." *Latin American Perspectives* 15, no. 2 (Spring), pp. 31–49.

Zimbalist, Andrew. 1988d. "Cuba." In *Struggle Against Dependence*, edited by Eva Paus. Boulder, CO: Westview, pp. 169–192.

Zimbalist, Andrew. 1989. "Incentives and Planning in Cuba." *Latin American Research Review* 24 (1), pp. 65–94.

Zimbalist, Andrew, and Claes Brundenius. 1989. *The Cuban Economy: Measurement and Analysis of Socialist Performance.* Baltimore: The Johns Hopkins University Press.

Zimbalist, Andrew, and Susan Eckstein. 1987. "Patterns of Cuban Development: The First Twenty-Five Years." *World Development* 12, no. 1 (Jan.), pp. 5–22.

Zuaznabar, Ismael. 1986. *La economía Cubana en la década del 50.* Havana: Editorial de Ciencias Sociales.

# Index